About the Author

Born in Toronto in 1903, MORLEY CALLAGHAN is a graduate of the University of Toronto and of Osgoode Hall law school. He was called to the bar in 1928, the same year that his first novel, *Strange Fugitive*, was published, but he never practised; his part-time work as a cub reporter on the *Toronto Star* had infected him with the ambition to be a full-time writer.

Although he has travelled widely, and lived for some time in Paris during the golden years of Hemingway and Fitzgerald, Callaghan has spent most of his life in Toronto quietly producing a stream of novels and short stories that have gained him admiration around the world. In Canada he has won a host of honours, including the Governor General's Award for Fiction. In late 1982 he became a Companion of the Order of Canada. In 1983 his acclaimed novel *A Time for Judas* became a major best-seller, and his novel *Our Lady of the Snows* was published in 1985.

That Summer in Paris

That Summer in Paris

MORLEY CALLAGHAN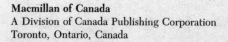

MEMORIES OF TANGLED FRIENDSHIPS
WITH HEMINGWAY, FITZGERALD,
AND SOME OTHERS

Macmillan Paperbacks 23

Macmillan of Canada
A Division of Canada Publishing Corporation
Toronto, Ontario, Canada

Canadian Cataloguing in Publication Data

Callaghan, Morley, date.
  That summer in Paris

(Macmillan paperbacks ; 23)
ISBN 0-7715-9270-1

1. Callaghan, Morley, date—Friends and
associates.   2. Hemingway, Ernest, 1899-1961—
Friends and associates.   3. Fitzgerald, F. Scott
(Francis Scott), 1896-1940—Friends and associates.   4. Novelists, Canadian (English)—
20th century—Biography.*   5. Novelists, American—20th century—Biography.   I. Title.

PS8505.A41Z53 1987   C818′.5203   C86-094815-3
PR9199.3.C34Z47 1987

Originally published in hardcover 1963 by The Macmillan
Company of Canada Limited under ISBN 0-7705-1419-7

First paperback edition 1973

First Laurentian Library edition (LL 40) 1976, ISBN 0-7715-9845-9

Reprinted 1981

First Macmillan Paperbacks edition 1987

Printed in Canada

That Summer in Paris

CHAPTER I

One September afternoon in 1960 I was having a drink with an old newspaper friend, Ken Jonstone, when unexpectedly he told me he had a message to pass on from Ronnie Jacques, the well-known New York photographer. Jacques had been in Sun Valley taking some pictures of Hemingway, and they had got to talking about me. After awhile, Hemingway, really opening up, had become warm and jovial. In the old days in Paris he used to box with me, he said. It had all been rather wonderful and amusing, Hemingway assured Ronnie, and there had been one ridiculous occasion when Scott Fitzgerald had acted as timekeeper, and everybody had been full of wine. Anyway, Hemingway sent his warmest regards. But what had really happened? Ken Jonstone wanted to know.

Shrugging, I made some lighthearted comment and didn't answer. Since I hadn't heard from Hemingway for years, I

was surprised. I suppose it made me meditative. Of course
it wasn't true that we had all been full of wine that afternoon
in Paris in 1929; yet come to think of it, maybe Ernest, even
years ago, had determinedly chosen to regard it in that light.
He could have made himself believe it, too.

As I sat at the bar with my friend hearing how Ernest had
recalled our Paris afternoons, I wondered why I wasn't more
deeply touched. No man had meant more to me than Ernest.
But in the years since those days he had gone far along another path. He had gone right out of my life. The Ernest I
had known so well had been the author of *A Farewell to
Arms, The Sun Also Rises,* and the early stories. Though I
had gone on reading his books he had become a public figure,
a man of legends, and I could hardly recognize in those
legends the man I had once known who had all my affection.
As for Fitzgerald, that charming and talented man—memories
of him had always aroused in me a half-guilty regret, a
twinge of shame.

So the secondhand greeting from Ernest only made me
wonder and smile. It didn't put me in a sentimental mood.
Anyway, I was now feeling confident and sure of myself. In
the last ten years I had written *The Loved and the Lost, The
Many Colored Coat* and was finishing *A Passion in Rome.*
What Hemingway might have thought of any of these books,
or whether he had even read one of them, had ceased to matter to me.

It was the following summer when a man from one of the
wire services telephoned and told me that Hemingway was
dead. I couldn't believe it. After a pause I said, "Don't worry,
he'll turn up again." The newspaperman insisted that Hemingway had blown his head off with a shotgun. Walking out
to my wife I said, "Hemingway is dead." "Oh, no," she said.

"He can't be." Even though we hadn't really talked about him for years we assumed that he would always be secure in some place in some other country strutting around, or making a fool of himself, or writing something beautiful. Now it was like hearing that the Empire State Building had fallen down —a nine-day wonder; but at the time I was shocked rather than sorrowful and I went around saying, "If that was the way he wanted it . . ." or, "If he knew he was sick and deteriorating it would have been unbearable to him." No man could have sounded more objective than I. A month passed, I would be out walking with my wife and suddenly I would remember something Hemingway had said in the Paris days. Or something Fitzgerald had said about Hemingway. One night she said to me, "Do you know you're talking about Fitzgerald and Hemingway all the time now? Why is it?"

"Well, isn't it strange that only last year he should have been talking to Ronnie Jacques in Sun Valley about those times with Fitzgerald and me in Paris in the summer of '29?" That night I couldn't sleep. Little scenes from our lives in the Quarter in Paris kept dancing in my mind. That Raspail and Montparnasse corner would light up brightly with the cafés crowded and the headwaiters shaking hands with the regular patrons. Or down at the Deux Magots I could see Fitzgerald coming to meet me with his elegant and distinguished air. And in the oak-paneled Falstaff, Jimmy behind the bar, and Hemingway coming in, looking lonely, then his face lighting up with his quick sweet smile when he saw us, friends he could feel free to sit down with. It was all too vivid in my mind.

Going to a desk drawer I hadn't opened for years I rummaged around through some old letters. And there was the one from Scott, written from Paris, dated January 1, 1930.

It began: "Dear Morley, I apologize unreservedly for having sent you that stupid and hasty telegram . . ." and then the line, "I have never mentioned the matter to Perkins or Edmund Wilson. . . ." Perkins at that time was his editor at Scribner's and mine and Ernest's too. But Wilson seemed to be the one who was Scott's good conscience about writers and writing. How odd it was to come across this line in the old letter! A few years ago I had told Wilson some of the facts in this story. . . . And then Scott's concluding line: "I will gladly make amends to anyone concerned, or to you in person on my return in February."

Poor Scott, with all his talent and all his fine sensibility, forever managing to be the one who got himself into a bad light no matter how honorable his intentions. When he wrote that letter to me something had ended forever between him and Ernest.

Still rummaging through disordered papers I found the letters from Ernest. When I had read them I was full of profound regret. Looking back on it over so many years, Ernest, laughing jovially, had been able to see the thing in a happy perspective—happy for him. But how do I know? Being Ernest, he could have known from the beginning he hadn't needed Scott's close friendship and admiration. Even before the trouble I had seen him resisting Scott. As for me—why did I never get in touch with Ernest again? Nor he with me—not personally, anyway. He could say, "Well, I never heard from you, not even when I won the Nobel prize." It was true. So I sat there for some hours brooding over those old letters, remembering how desperately important it had once been to me to get to Paris and enjoy the friendship of Scott and Ernest.

CHAPTER II

I have to tell how Paris came to have such importance as a place for me, and if possible, what I was like too in those days. It can only be done by telling where I was and what I was doing in 1923 when I was twenty and in my second year at College in Toronto. Five foot eight, with dark brown curly hair and blue eyes, I was not overweight then. I was fast with my tongue and, under pressure, fast with my fists, but they tell me that I moved around rather lazily. At college I played football and boxed. For years I had played baseball in the city sandlot leagues. That summer in the holidays my cousin got me a job in a lumberyard "slugging" lumber with five husky immigrant laborers. We unloaded six-by-two scantling from boxcars. At the time, I was also reading wildly. I read Dostoevski, Joseph Conrad, Sinclair Lewis, Flaubert; *The Dial, The Adelphi,* and the old *Smart Set,*

edited by H. L. Mencken and George Jean Nathan; Catherine
Mansfield. D. H. Lawrence—everything. Yet in the summer
it was baseball that absorbed me. I was a pitcher. My
brother, a catcher on the same team, was a singer, bent on
studying opera. Our ball team, a very good one, one of the
best in the city, had some rough tough players with a rich
fine flow of language who were not concerned with my interest in Conrad and Dostoevski or my brother's beautiful
voice—only in my curve ball and my brother's batting aver-
age. After I had been working two weeks in the lumberyard,
my turn came to pitch a game. In the first inning I noticed
that my arm felt unusually light; coming around on the pitch
it felt weightless, and yet I had no speed. "To hell with that
lumberyard," I said.

A friend of my boyhood, Art Kent, had a job reporting on
a morning paper. Sometimes at night, for the sake of his
company, I had gone with him on his assignments. Reporting, I told myself, would be much easier on a pitching arm
than slugging lumber, so I paid a visit to the Toronto *Daily
Star*. The elderly gentleman at the reception desk, impressed
by my earnestness, and believing I had a big story to report
to the city editor, called a Mr. Harry Johnston. This stocky,
plump, long-nosed man with hair graying at the temples and
a deliberately alert manner, came out to the desk and said
brusquely, "The city editor, Mr. Hindmarsh, is on his holidays. I'm Mr. Johnston. What is it, young fellow?" I told him
I was from the university and was a very good reporter and
wanted a job. The disgusted expression on his face as he
looked at the old gentleman abashed me. "We're not hiring
anybody. I'm busy," he said. But when he opened the city
room door I followed. With a knowing air that must have
carried a strong conviction I added urgently that a news-

paper could always use a good reporter, wasn't that right? As he half turned I said, "Let me work around here for a week. If at the end of the week you think I'm no good, don't pay me anything. Let me go. What have you got to lose?" A flicker of interest in his eyes, he said, "I'll think about it. Come in tomorrow," and he got away from me.

At the same hour next day I was back at the reception desk, expecting to be led into the editor's office. Instead, Mr. Johnston, now in his shirt sleeves and with an impatient air, came again to the hall desk. He was sorry, but they weren't taking on any more summer replacements. This time I walked right into the city room with him. "Look here," I insisted. "What I said yesterday must have sounded good or you wouldn't have told me to come back. If it was good yesterday isn't it good today? I'll work for nothing for a week. If I'm any good, keep me on and when the city editor comes back you have in me another pretty good reporter. What do you lose if it doesn't cost you anything?"

My effrontery had seemed to attract him. Smiling a little, he asked, "What's your name?" and he wrote it down. "You won't be on the salary list but come in at seven in the morning," and he walked away abruptly.

I had never been in a newsroom. This one had a row of desks running the length of the room and a big round city desk at which there were four deskmen. At seven in the morning Mr. Johnston was one of them. He hardly spoke to me. I sat down nervously. In a little while one of the deskmen came hurrying to me with a small sheaf of clippings from the morning newspaper. "Scalp these obituaries," he said. For two hours I rewrote obituaries.

When the assignment book was made up and brought out from the city editor's office, I gathered around it with the other reporters, my heart jumping. My name was there. I was to cover a druggists' convention at the King Edward Hotel, just along the street. Hurrying over to the hotel I found hundreds of druggists assembling in the lobby. Out of this morning assembly, I thought, I had to get a witty story about druggists and drugstores. Back in the city room I wrote in long hand what I was sure was an elegant and amusing story and handed it to a young deskman named Jimmy Cowan, who began to read it. I watched him drop the first page in the basket. The second page got only a glance from him. There was no change of expression on his face. As my pages one by one went into the basket I waited for him to speak derisively to Mr. Johnston. Instead, he simply went on with his work. I was so worried I could hardly eat any lunch. My druggists were getting down to business in the convention hall right after lunch.

At the reporters' table I found myself sitting beside an older man from the morning paper. Without any shame I told him how green I was. I told him I didn't know what kind of story to write or what to do, or even what was expected of me. A few "sticks" were needed for the afternoon edition, he said, and a few more for the later one. He even told me the deadlines of my own paper. An hour later, after glancing at his watch, he wrote two little paragraphs of hard cold news and told me to get it over to my city desk and come back. I didn't even bother rewriting the paragraphs. Two hours later I was back in the office with three more paragraphs in the same hand. That day I learned something I never forgot. Wherever I have been in the world and have wanted to know something or get something done I have gone to a newspaperman and confessed my utter ignorance, and have always been helped.

Whenever I think of Mr. Johnston now I think of those short legs of his in rapid motion. At the end of the week the legs moved rapidly in my direction, then stopped. "I've put you on the salary list at twenty a week," he said. I went to the telephone, called home and said quietly to my mother, "I got on the *Star*." "I knew you would, Son," she said. So I went out and loafed along King Street, nursing my delight and vaguely aware that I might be coming to a turning point in my life.

In those days the Toronto *Daily Star* was as aggressive and raffish a newspaper as you could find in any North American city. Its newsroom was the kind of a place Napoleon must have had in mind when he spoke of a career open to talent and ambition. It had a promotion department that went in for baby elephants, balloons and Santa Claus funds. *Star* reporters moved on great disasters in far places like shock troops poured into a breach by an excited general. A reporter might get a quick salary increase or be fired promptly. Since I didn't have a family to support, or a mortgage to pay off, I loved this turbulent arena. In the freebooting society of our room each man was intent on looking after himself and I got two salary increases in a month.

One day on the street I had encountered an older man I had known in a YMCA when I had been in high school. He was a good earnest likable man. How astounded I was to learn from him that he had become the secretary of the newly formed Communist party of Canada. We looked at each other and laughed. I called him a dirty Red; he called me a cheap hireling of the dirty capitalist press. Yet he said he might have stories for me if I didn't distort them. For example, W. Z. Foster, the leader of the American Communist party, was being smuggled into Canada that weekend to make a speech. Would I like to meet Foster, who was crashing the immigration barrier? Hurrying back to my Mr. Johnston, I electrified him, telling him Foster would be in Toronto and I would be led to him by an emissary who would meet me at a street corner on Saturday night at nine.

"Good, good," said Harry, his eyes shining. "Our Mr. Reade will be there. You take our Mr. Reade with you. It's a scoop, a great story." Our Mr. Reade, a man about twenty years older than I, a Rhodes scholar, wrote all the fancy special stories.

On Saturday night I appeared at the street meeting, and while listening to revolutionary speeches, I circled warily around the crowd. But of couse I was such an unimportant figure on the paper that our Mr. Reade couldn't be expected to know me. I was supposed to know him. Everyone on the *Star* was expected to know Bobby Reade. Then a young Communist whom I had never seen before grabbed my arm. "You're Morley Callaghan, aren't you? Come on." And he took me to a store about a mile away along King Street and in the back room with his devotees was W. Z. Foster. I spent the whole evening with him. Afterward I went back to the city room, worked all night on the story, then went home.

My mother had left a note for me: *Call Mr. Johnston,* but by that time it was nearly dawn. I went to bed. At nine the phone rang and it was Harry Johnston. "Why didn't you meet Mr. Reade?" he shouted angrily. I said, "I was there. Why wasn't Mr. Reade there?" But he screamed, "Mr. Reade was there," and I said, "Why didn't Mr. Reade speak to me?" and he yelled, "Mr. Reade says he doesn't know you." And I yelled, "What makes Mr. Reade think I should know him? The story is in your box." "It is? Well, we'll see," he said threateningly. "A *Star* man doesn't have to be told things,

Callaghan. If he can't pick up things in a week, a simple thing like knowing who our Mr. Reade is, we don't want him around." And he hung up. But when I went into the office on Monday he told me he had put me down for a five-dollar raise. Only then did he introduce me to the scholarly Mr. Reade.

I was getting along. In the mornings there was the hotel beat, and loafing from hotel to hotel, in the hope of encountering a visitor who might make a good interview, my thoughts were usually on writing. Visitors to the hotels might be strange characters I could use in stories. Why did I dislike so much contemporary writing? I would wonder. The popular writers of the day like Hergesheimer, Edith Wharton, James Branch Cabell, Galsworthy, Hugh Walpole, H. G. Wells—except for *Tono Bungay*—I had rejected fiercely. Show-off writers; writers intent on proving to their readers that they could be clever and had some education, I would think. Such vanities should be beneath them if they were really concerned in revealing the object as it was. Those lines, *A primrose by a river's brim a yellow primrose was to him, and it was nothing more,* often troubled me, aroused my anger. What the hell else did Wordsworth want it to be? An orange? A sunset? I would ask myself, Why does one thing have to remind you of something else? Going from hotel to hotel on my job I would brood over it.

I remember deciding that the root of the trouble with writing was that poets and storywriters used language to evade, to skip away from the object, because they could never bear to face the thing freshly and see it freshly for what it was in itself. A kind of double talk; one thing always seen in terms of another thing. Criticism? A dreary metaphor. The whole academic method! Of course there were lines like *Life's but a walking shadow.* . . . Just the same, I'd be damned if the glory of literature was in the metaphor. Besides, it was not a time for the decorative Renaissance flight into simile. Tell the truth cleanly. Weren't the consequences of fraudulent pretending plain to anyone who would look around? Hadn't the great slogans of the first World War become ridiculous to me before I had left high school? Wilsonian idealism! Always the flight of fancy. And Prohibition. Another fantasy. It was hilarious, a beautiful example of the all-prevailing fraudulent morality; and at college it had become a social obligation to go to a bootlegger's, and a man came to have a sneaking respect for those who openly broke the law—not for the policeman standing on a corner.

And the philosophy of St. Thomas Aquinas which I got in my college classroom? All the big words, the metaphysics, were to be treated with grudging suspicion. Nothing could be taken for granted. Nothing could be taken on authority. A craving for authority had led to Prohibition and stupid censorship in Boston. Orthodoxy was for fat comfortable inert people who agreed to pretend, agreed to accept the general fraud, the escape into metaphor. All around me seemed to be some kind of a wild energy that could be tapped and controlled. In the dance halls I heard the jazz sounds coming from Chicago. That town, Chicago! The bootleggers, the shootings, the open disrespect for all that had been thought of as socially acceptable. And Sherwood Anderson and Carl Sandburg had lived in Chicago.

Yet Chicago didn't beckon to me. Nor did Greenwich Village. Edna Millay, Eugene O'Neill, Floyd Dell, Max Bodenheim. I knew all the names. But the Village seemed to me to be a place full of characters. I was against all writers who wanted to become "characters." The whole contemporary world was full of characters. Women rode on the wings of airplanes, men sat on flagpoles, there were stunt men of all kinds, jazz musicians, young ladies going gallantly to hell on bathtub gin. But there was also the way Jack Dempsey fought. His brutal mauling style seemed to be telling me something: do the thing you want to do in your own way. Be excellent at it. Seek your own excellence. Having no use for pure aesthetes or aloof intellectuals, I went on playing ball, and enjoyed the skill required of a pitcher working on a hitter. I tell this to show the kind of thinking, the thoughts about writing, of a young reporter doing the hotel beat. In the hotels I sat talking far too long with opera singers or visiting senators.

In the hotel one day I remember encountering a British author, a nice middle-aged gray-haired man. And in no time I was telling him firmly that writing had to do with the right relationship between the words and the thing or person being described: the words should be as transparent as glass, and every time a writer used a brilliant phrase to prove himself witty or clever he merely took the mind of the reader away from the object and directed it to himself; he became simply a performer. Why didn't he go on the stage? The elderly British writer, regarding me thoughtfully, asked me how old I was. "An interesting view of style. Look here," and he took a page out of his notebook and wrote on it his name and the address of an English publisher. If I ever wrote anything I was to send this note along with it to the English publisher.

I remember one time at twilight, sitting at the typewriter in the sunroom of my parents' home. I could smell the lilacs. A night bird cried. A woman's voice came from a neighbor's yard. I wanted to get it down so directly that it wouldn't

feel or look like literature. I remembered too being with a
girl one night, and on the way home, walking alone, I felt
the world had been brought close to me; there seemed to be
magic in the sound of my own footsteps, even in the noise
of the streetcars—all mingled with the girl's kiss, the memory
of the little run I had noticed in her stocking, the way she
said good-bye to me. None of it had to be written up. There
it was, beautiful in itself. A "literary guy" would spoil it.

I was not at all lonely. I liked my father, mother and
brother, and felt under no compulsion to leave home. I liked
the university and had learned there that if I just passed my
exams, no professor could get on my back and I had time to
get my own education. I loved working on the *Star*, went to
the dance hall, always had a girl.

In my city were many poets, a group of painters called the
Group of Seven, and no doubt many great readers and
scholars. But in those days it was a very British city. I was
intensely North American. It never occurred to me that the
local poets had anything to do with me. Physically, and with
some other part of me, the ball-playing, political, debating,
lovemaking, family part of me, I was wonderfully at home
in my native city, and yet intellectually, spiritually, the part
that had to do with my wanting to be a writer was utterly,
but splendidly and happily, alien. It was something like this:
my father had no interest in baseball; I never bothered him
about it; he never bothered me about it. That was the way it
was with me as a student, a young reporter interested in his
own view of writing in this city. If I had to become a lawyer,
all right, I would practice law. And then I met our real city
editor, the fearsome Mr. Hindmarsh, who had come back
from his holidays.

I have to tell you about this man, Harry Hindmarsh. If it

hadn't been for Hindmarsh, Hemingway might have remained a year in Toronto, he might not have written *The Sun Also Rises*, and I might have settled into newspaper work. Hindmarsh was the grand antagonist. But I never hated him as Hemingway did. There was always some sardonic humor in my view of him. All the duels with him really pushed me closer to Paris. Hemingway maintained that Hindmarsh was a bad newspaperman. It wasn't true. Hindmarsh was a hard-driving, good, ruthless newspaperman. But as the general of the *Star* army, always on the move, he had some failings. Perhaps it wasn't such an advantage to him after all that he had married the daughter of the president of the Star Publishing Company, Joseph Atkinson. Perhaps it had something to do with his refusal to permit any one of his employees to enjoy his own sense of security. With his anger, childish petulance and inexplicable moodiness, he seemed to be driven to break any proud man's spirit. And yet he was sentimental. He was capable of gusts of inexplicable moody kindness. When a man was really broken, an alcoholic or a debt-ridden fool or some other lost soul, helpless and on his knees, Hindmarsh would be there with a helping hand, saying in effect, "Rise, my son, I am with you. Let me look after things for you."

One morning Hindmarsh, accompanied by his assistant Johnston, came walking along the aisle from the city desk past the row of reporters' desks on his way to his office. The big heavy-shouldered man with close-cropped hair and an assured, dominating manner, stopped in front of me. Astonished, I stood up slowly. "Mr. Callaghan," said my Mr. Johnston, "meet Mr. Hindmarsh." I put out my hand warily, but the big fellow was smiling at me benevolently.

"You were hired as a summer replacement," he said.

"Yes, Mr. Hindmarsh," and I saw that Mr. Johnston, who had gambled and hired me, was not looking unhappy.

"Well, my boy," said Mr. Hindmarsh, with a surprisingly warm grin, "I understand you wrote that story about W. Z. Foster. I have decided you're cut out to be a newspaperman. You can join the permanent staff."

Embarrassed, I told him I hadn't finished my university course and would have to go back to college.

Whirling on my Mr. Johnston, Hindmarsh growled, "I thought you told me this man was a varsity graduate?"

"Mr. Callaghan, didn't you tell me you were a graduate?" asked Johnston, and I saw by the expression on his face that he was scared stiff of Hindmarsh. "You didn't ask me," I said nervously. "Nobody asked me."

"Nobody asked you?" and Mr. Hindmarsh, grunting, drew back and brooded over both me and Mr. Johnston, then shook his head sadly.

"I assumed . . ." began Mr. Johnston nervously. But then Mr. Hindmarsh half smiled. "Never mind," he said. "Go back to college. Graduate. We'll work something out for you to keep you on the paper." As Mr. Hindmarsh strode away Mr. Johnston remained studying me with a perplexed air. But I hurried out. My God, I thought, what will Hindmarsh say when he discovers that I have still another year to go at college?

By this time that thin, whispering deskman, Jimmy Cowan, the only one I talked to about writing, would pass on to me bits of local gossip in his sinister mutter. Cowan read all the American writers, kept track of Mencken in the old *Smart Set*, could talk about the Greenwich Village crowd, and even read the theatrical paper, *Variety*. One day, near the end of summer, he whispered to me, his eye rolling around the newsroom as if he had to make sure no one was listening, "A good newspaperman is coming from Europe to join the staff. Our European correspondent, Ernest Hemingway." Then he told me that Hemingway had been in Toronto some four years ago when he had done some work for the *Star Weekly*. Since I had never heard of this Mr. Hemingway I could only say "Oh."

A few weeks later, one noontime, crossing the street to the *Star* building, I saw a tall, broad-shouldered, brown-eyed, high-colored man with a heavy black mustache coming out of the building. He was wearing a peak cap. He smiled at me politely. He had a quick, eager, friendly smile and looked like a Latin. No Toronto newspaperman would be wearing that peak cap, and I knew he must be the new man from Europe, Ernest Hemingway.

Next morning when the assignment book was brought from H. C. Hindmarsh's office and the reporters gathered around, I ran my eye down the page and saw Hemingway's name in at least five places. Fascinated, I looked to see what kind of assignment was being given the big correspondent from Europe. Five inconsequential jobs such as I might be asked to do myself! While I stood there Hemingway came in, looked at the book, muttered a terse four-letter word and hurried out white-faced. I could see what was happening. Our Mr. Hindmarsh was determined that no one should get the impression that he was going to be coddled. But Hemingway's startled curse, muttered over my shoulder, was the only word I heard from him for over a month.

In those weeks I don't think I saw him more than once or twice, for he was busy galloping around the country in the Hindmarsh harness. But I had heard—I was always hearing things about him—that he'd brought from Paris a book of his called *Three Stories and Ten Poems,* privately printed. My friend Jimmy Cowan loaned me this book for one night. I can remember being in the city room long after midnight, finishing up an assignment, and across from me sat two older, learned and well-paid colleagues. I couldn't resist asking them if they had read *Three Stories and Ten Poems.* They had. And what did they think of it? Their supercilious contempt enraged me. When I argued with them, they dismissed me good-humoredly. After all, they didn't even know my name. I can still remember the patient smile of the older one as he said, "Remember this, my boy. Three swallows never made a summer."

"All right, I think he's a great writer," I said belligerently. "Now just wait and see."

So far I hadn't even shaken hands with Hemingway, and yet I would pick up bits of information about him. He had a peculiar and, for him, I think, fatal quality. He made men want to talk about him. He couldn't walk down the street and stub his toe without having a newspaperman who happened to be walking with him magnify the little accident into a near fatality. How he was able to get these legends going I still don't know. But I would hear of the dramatic tension developing between him and Mr. Hindmarsh. How magnified all this was I can't say. I do say, even in those days everything that was happening to Hemingway was magnified by someone. I heard that he had hardly time to be with his wife, Hadley, when she was having her baby. And yet he was suddenly moved downstairs to enjoy the leisurely life on the *Star Weekly.*

At this time I went back to school for the fall term. But three times a week I would come down to the editorial room where I got my assignment, then I would go downstairs to the library and sit writing my story. One afternoon I looked up and there was Hemingway, watching me. I imagine he had time on his hands and was looking for someone to talk to. Though years have passed I still wonder what brought him to me.

He was sitting across from me, leaning close, and there was real sweetness in his smile and a wonderful availability, and he made me feel that he was eagerly and deeply involved in everything. We began to talk. He told me that he had come to Toronto because his wife was having a baby and he had heard Toronto doctors were very good. As soon as possible, he said vehemently, he'd go back to Paris. He couldn't write in Toronto. There is a story that while he was in Toronto he was sending out stories to the little magazines in Paris. This is nonsense. Those Paris magazines, the *Transatlantic Review, transition, This Quarter* and Ezra Pound's *Exile* hadn't even been launched.

He had come to Toronto with good expectations, and now he seemed to feel smothered, though he had good friends here. I could see it wasn't only the job that was bothering him. I didn't know what it was. Yet he had a strange and delightful candor, and every time I looked at his warm, dark face with the restless eyes I liked him more.

Words came from him not in an eloquent flow but with a quiet, tense authority. He gave me a quick rundown on the talents of the better-known reporters. This one was "a good newspaperman." Another one—"There's no one better at the kind of thing he's doing." But with some he was brutal. "Him? He simply has no shame." This one had a homosexual style. Then we began to talk about literature. All his judgments seemed to come out of an intense and fierce conviction, but he offered them to you as if he were letting you in on something. "James Joyce is the greatest writer in the world," he said. *Huckleberry Finn* was a very great book. Had I read Stendahl? Had I read Flaubert? Always appearing to be sharing a secret; yet watching me intently. He seemed pleased that I was so approving of the intention behind the great Stendahl style. And there was Melville; if I was interested in symbolism, *Moby Dick* was the great work. And what did I think of Stephen Crane? Did I agree that *The Red Badge of Courage* was a great war book? I was to wonder about his enthusiasm for *The Red Badge of Courage*, especially when, later on, he made such a point about a writer needing to experience for himself the scenes he described. Crane's book was a work purely of the imagination.

Suddenly he asked how old I was, and I told him, and he said he was seven years older. Then he said solemnly, "You know, you are very intelligent."

"Well, thanks," I said uncomfortably, for people I knew in Toronto didn't say such things to each other.

"Do you write fiction?" he asked.

"A little."

"Have you got a story around?"

"As a matter of fact, I have."

"When do you come down here again?"

"On Friday."

"Bring the story along," he said. "I'll look for you," and he got up and left.

But my Friday assignment took me out of the office. The following Monday afternoon I passed Hemingway on the stairs. Wheeling suddenly four steps above me, looming over me, big and powerful, he growled, "You didn't bring that story down."

"No, I was busy."

"I see," he said, then rude and brutal, he added, "I just wanted to see if you were another god-damned phony."

His brutal frankness shocked me, and I felt my face burning. "I'm retyping the story," I said curtly. "I'll bring it down. Don't worry. I'll be in there Wednesday at three."

"We'll see," he said, and as he hurried up the stairs, anyone watching would probably have thought I owed him some money and had been ducking him.

On Wednesday I was waiting in the library with my story, and within five minutes Hemingway appeared. He had some proofs in his hand. "Did you bring the story?" he asked. I handed it to him. "I brought these along," he said, handing me the proofs. They were the proofs of the first edition of *In Our Time*, the little book done in Paris on special paper with hand-set type. "I'll read your story," he said, "and you read these."

We sat across from each other at the table, reading, and not a word was said. His work was just a series of long paragraphs, little vignettes. They were so polished they were like epigrams, each paragraph so vivid, clean and intense that the scene he was depicting seemed to dance before my eyes. Sitting there I knew I was getting a glimpse of the work of a great writer.

When he saw that I had finished with his proofs he put down my story and said quietly, "You're a real writer. You write big-time stuff. All you have to do is keep on writing."

He spoke so casually, but with such tremendous authority, that I suddenly couldn't doubt him. Without knowing it, I was in the presence of that authority he evidently had to have to hold his life together. He had to believe he knew, as I found out later, or he was lost. Whether it was in the field of boxing, or soldiering, or bullfighting or painting, he had to believe he was the one who knew. And he could make people believe he did, too. "Now what about my proofs?" he asked. Fumbling a little, and not sounding like a critic, I told him how impressed I was. "What do your friends in Paris say about this work?" I asked.

"Ezra Pound says it is the best prose he has read in forty years," he said calmly.

At that time the poet Ezra Pound was not a big name in Toronto, but to young writers in English, whether they lived in New York, Paris or London, he was the prophet, the great discoverer, the man of impeccable taste. I think I saw then why Hemingway wanted to get out of Toronto like a bat out of hell. He had a kind of frantic pride, and though he had good friends among his colleagues in Toronto, they couldn't imagine they were in the presence of a man who was writing the best prose that had been written in the last forty years. Was that why he said to me so firmly, "Whatever you do, don't let anyone around here tell you anything"?

From then on, whenever I came down to the *Star* I would wait around in the library and often Hemingway would show up and we would talk about writers and writing. My life was taking a new turn in those encounters, for at last I had found a dedicated artist to talk to. He would say such things as, "A writer is like a priest. He has to have the same feeling about his work." Another time he said, "Even if your father is dying and you are there at his side and heartbroken you have to be noting every little thing going on, no matter how much it hurts." Words wouldn't pour out of him; sometimes he would talk haltingly as if he stuttered. But he made me feel that he was willing to be ruthless with himself or with anything or anybody that got in the way of the perfection of his work.

Yes, at that time the dedicated artist, but not the big personality. I think at that time he would have scoffed at the notion of ever becoming such a big public personality for people who hardly knew his work. And as for me—I couldn't even imagine him ever letting it happen to him. The work was the thing, he seemed to say with every gesture. When I think of some of those absurd pictures I've seen of him in these last few years, or recall now how he went in for that Indian talk, one-syllable grunts, my mind goes back to those conversations years ago in the *Star* library.

What seems incredible now, almost mysterious, is that we would talk about Sherwood Anderson, James Joyce, Ezra Pound and Scott Fitzgerald—then at the height of his fame—all far away from me in Toronto, and yet it turned out that we were talking about people I was to know and be with in a few short years.

I was the one who mentioned Fitzgerald. I had been reading him in the Hart House library at college. I was dazzled by his quick success. Some of his stories meant nothing to me at all. But I had just read "The Diamond As Big As the Ritz." I had liked it. I had begun to wonder about him. I said I thought *This Side of Paradise* too literary a production, yet it was bright and fresh and engaging. Ernest seemed to be on the fence about that early Fitzgerald work. Not grudging, but somewhat dubious about the direction Fitzgerald might take. But he did make it clear that Fitzgerald wasn't exciting him at all. There in the library, talking so dispassionately, so judicially about Scott, how could we have imagined that a little time would pass and we would be with Scott, and our lives would become tangled in a swirl of fierce passions and wounded pride?

I remember our last conversation before he went away. When we met in the afternoon he asked me if I had a copy of his *Three Stories and Ten Poems*. I hadn't. At that time there was a little bookstore at Bay and Bloor where Hemingway had left some copies. "Let's walk up there," he said. It was a long walk and we loafed along slowly, absorbed in our conversation. I remember we were talking about the great Russian, Dostoevski, and I said, "The way he writes—it's like a forest fire. It sweeps indiscriminately over everything."

"That's pretty good," he said, pondering. Then he stopped on the street. "You know Harry Greb," he said, referring to the wonderful middleweight champion with the windmill style. "Well, Dostoevski writes like Harry Greb fights," he said. "He swarms all over you. Like this." And there on the street he started shadowboxing.

We got his little book from the bookshop, then walked over to Yonge and Bloor for a coffee. He wrote in the book, *To Callaghan with best luck and predictions,* and while he was doing it I said wrily that now he was going away it looked as if I was losing my reading public of one—him. "No," he said. "Remember this. There are always four or five people, somewhere in the world, who are interested in good new writing. Some magazines are starting up in Paris," and he sounded like a bishop and again I believed I only needed to wait.

On his last day at the *Star* I went down to the *Weekly* and walked in boldly to say good-bye to him. I remember he was sitting with the three top writers of the *Star Weekly:* Greg Clark, who was his friend, Charlie Vining and Fred Griffin. As I approached Hemingway to say good-bye, these three men looked at me in surprise, for they didn't even know me.

"Write and let me know how you're doing and as soon as

you get anything done, shoot it to Paris," he said. "I'll tell them about you."

"I've got your address. I'll see you in Paris."

"Care of the Guaranty Trust. That's right."

As I shook hands with him my face was burning, for I knew the others were looking at me in some wonder.

CHAPTER III

I didn't doubt that I would hear from him and see him again. It was just a feeling of certainty. With great confidence I began to write stories. At the university I found a student named Tom Murtha, who was interested in Dorothy Richardson and Katherine Mansfield. This student, a shy, talented man, was not given to the expression of much enthusiasm, but I could talk to him on even terms about my friend Hemingway, and show him what I was writing myself. Of an afternoon I would go down to the *Star* building and into the *Weekly* office and ask Greg Clark if he could go across the road to Childs and have a coffee. Greg Clark, a little man with a wonderful strut, a lot of charm, and shrewd gray eyes, had been a fine soldier in the war. He had a kind of big-brother sympathetic friendliness. Sometimes Jimmy Cowan would join us for a coffee and we would talk about Hemingway and wonder what he was doing, then Greg would start telling his own war stories. Years later I found that Greg could never remember anything I said to him, sitting in Childs. How could it have been otherwise? He was never listening to me. My confidence about writing amused him, but when I would show him a story, written on *Star* copy paper, he would lean back meditating. "I don't know. How do I know? Well, maybe Hem would like it," and I would know he thought it was unprintable. We were both laughing at each other, yet the wonderful thing about him was that he was the only man I knew on the newspaper who was willing to admit that possibly, just possibly, someone else in the world might think I was doing something very good.

When I had written a ten-thousand-word story about a young fellow's first love affair, I sent it to Paris. A month passed. No word came. It didn't matter. I never doubted the intensity of Ernest's interest. And I had found someone to whom I could communicate his faith in me. At a college dance I met Loretto. She had brown eyes and black hair and a Renaissance profile, and she had the advantage of not being steeped in bad writing. I remember the night I met her downtown, the night when I came hurrying to the street corner where she stood under the streetlight, and I whipped out a letter from Paris. Just a few lines on the page written in a small cramped hand, but signed by Ford Madox Ford. My story, shown to him by Hemingway, he wrote, was too long for the *Transatlantic Review* which he was editing in Paris, but could I send him something shorter? I was full of joy and excitement. Taking Loretto's arm, I hurried her along the street, telling her Ford was a great man in English letters, the collaborator of Joseph Conrad. "Didn't Hemingway say he would tell them in Paris about me?" I said. "Well, he's telling them." Crossing in front of the Catholic cathedral I stopped suddenly. "I'll go to Paris. I'll take you with me," I said. Laughing, not quite believing me, she asked how I could get to Paris if I studied law. But that night I knew in my heart that I had touched the world beyond my hometown. In Toronto, Paris indeed became my city of light.

CHAPTER IV

But Hemingway's privately printed Three Mountain Press edition of *In Our Time,* just the short paragraphs, had come out. Each day I looked through the revues for some notice of the work. Finally I found one of those shorter notices in H. L. Mencken's *American Mercury.* The note said: . . . *written in the bold bad manner of the Café Dôme.* This derisive little notice enraged me. "Who told Mencken to print those stories of Anderson's, I wonder?" I said jeeringly to Loretto. "Someone must have told him. Left to himself, Mencken obviously has no feeling for what is new and good."

Summer came, and I was back on the *Star.* When I wrote a story called "A Girl With Ambition" and sent it to Paris, Hemingway answered at once. A first-class story, he said, and he urged me to do more and let him see them. Boni and Liveright were bringing out a trade edition of *In Our Time* which would have some longer stories between the short paragraphs I had seen, he wrote. I sent him another story called, "Last Spring They Came Over," and he wrote me that he had known at the beginning I would do such stories. Let him see anything else I did and he would keep on passing the word around about me. In these letters he would tell me little about what he was doing himself. I seemed to be writing more stories than he was. Imagine my pride when he wrote me that Tolstoy couldn't have done my "Wedding Dress" story any better! I was always elated, always excited in those days. Whenever I got one of these letters from him I would go down to the *Weekly* and see my friend Greg Clark or some of the other older newsmen. They couldn't figure out why Hemingway was writing to me from Paris. My friend Greg had made some comment on one of my stories and when I told it to Ernest he wrote me that Greg was the "most wonderful guy in the world," but I was never to let him tell me about anything. Each letter, each passing month, seemed to take me a little closer to Paris where my friend now had my stories.

Sometimes at night, after leaving Loretto, I would go home to my parents' house, read Tolstoy in bed for an hour, then begin to dream that there would be a letter from Paris in the morning telling me that some distinguished editor, having spent the night reading all my stories, wanted to hear from me.

When Hemingway's book *In Our Time* came out in New York, I remember picking up a copy of the *Saturday Review of Literature* in which there was a review by the editor, Henry Seidel Canby, with the heading, "Art On It's Last Legs." I threw it down in disgust.

Writing to Ernest I told him I had got a piddling little six-inch notice of the book in a local paper. Avoid reviewing books, he wrote me. It was all right to talk about a writer if you had to, but always remember that you can't run with the hares and hunt with the hounds.

At the end of that second summer on the *Star*, Mr. Hindmarsh called me into his office. "All right, Callaghan, now that you are to be on the permanent staff—" he began.

"I'm sorry, Mr. Hindmarsh," I said meekly. "I have another year to go at college before I graduate."

"What do you mean? You failed your year?"

"No, I got through all right."

"You assured me last year you had one year more."

"I said I had to go back. Nobody ever asked me what year I was in at any time."

I had put him in the position I had put Mr. Johnston in; it was intolerable to him and he regarded me sourly. Johnston would laugh. Then fairly enough he may have recalled that he, too, had forgotten to ask me what year I had been in at college. Never had I met a man who had such a devastating scowl. But he finally grunted at me, "Are you now definitely in your graduating year at college?"

"I am, Mr. Hindmarsh."

"When you go back this time we won't pay you any salary. We'll pay you space rates. You can come down here three times a week to get your assignment. After thanking him, I got away quickly.

I had a good year at college, going to Pittsburgh with the debating team. But Hemingway, hearing of it, wrote me that I should leave debating to men like Main Johnston, a *Star* editorial writer. But then, as I knew, Hemingway himself often seemed to have a little stutter, and I smiled to myself. Having finished my final examination, I reported to

Mr. Hindmarsh, who was sitting at the city desk. Turning to me he said with too much grim satisfaction, "All right, Callaghan. You're on the permanent staff now. Well, you need discipline, the routine assignments. Now I'm going to put you to harness."

He might just as well have grabbed me by the arm, shouting, "I've got you now, you little bastard. You've no place else to go." And I retreated, muttering to myself, "If that guy thinks he's putting me in his damned harness he's crazy."

A comical period on the *Star* had begun for me. Trying on the harness for size, I went to the summer courts at Osgoode Hall. In summer, of course, the courts were hardly in session. It was a nothing job. Nothing to do but wait around until judgments were handed down. The other court reporters, older men enjoying the quiet life, took turns sleeping on the table in the reporters' room or playing checkers. In this company, as Mr. Hindmarsh saw it, I was supposed to bite my nails, dream of being restored to his imperial favor, dream of great assignments. Well, instead I dreamt of Paris. In my exile I sat at the typewriter working on stories to send to Paris. Even the legal judgments handed down in the summer I read as if they were case books on human nature. I would come back to the city room quietly, hoping I wouldn't be noticed, and with hardly a glance at Mr. Hindmarsh, slip away. If he gave me a small story of another kind to do, a piece of reporting, I would take great pains with the writing, practicing my own prose, trying to be exact and get a certain rhythm. Of course to do this I had to avoid all the bright showy gestures that were supposed to mark the work of an ambitious young reporter anxious to attract the attention of Mr. Hindmarsh.

One day he called me to the city desk. "I know what's the

matter with you," he said sourly. "You're sore, aren't you?"

"You're wrong, Mr. Hindmarsh. I'm not sore. What am I supposed to be sore about?"

"I'm not wrong," he said sharply. "Don't tell me I'm wrong. You're sore because I have you over there in Osgoode Hall. You think you should be getting sixty dollars a week and writing all the big stories on the paper. Well, I'm breaking you in. You'll get into harness just like anybody else. You might as well get used to it."

It was his custom, when coming in in the morning, to walk the length of all the desks on his way to his office. On the way he would smile and nod to each reporter, who would say brightly, "Good morning, Mr. Hindmarsh." All the quick, bright, alert "good morning, Mr. Hindmarshes" would ring in his ears as he moved heavily into his office. One morning his secretary, Ernie, came to me. "Mr. Hindmarsh wants to see you," he said. The big fellow, lonely and brooding, was slumped in his chair. Finally I seemed to come under his eyes, but he waited till I grew embarrassed, then snapped at me, "What's the matter with you, Callaghan? There's something the matter with you."

"You're wrong, Mr. Hindmarsh."

"Don't contradict me," he said petulantly. "When I come in in the morning I expect a cheerful good morning from the men. What do I get from you?" he asked bitterly. "Every morning when I come in I have to look at your sullen face." My sullen face troubling such a dominating figure? What a man. He sounded so much like a petulant boy it was embarrassing. Then he went on, "I'm tired of your sullen face."

"That's all wrong, Mr. Hindmarsh . . ." I began.

"Don't you stand here in my own office telling me I'm wrong," he shouted. "Get out of here. You're fired!"

Startled, mute, I backed away from him, but when I got to the door he seemed to relent. "Just a minute," he said and I remember I had to wait as he got up and stood looking out the window. His face showed anger, concern, resentment; he looked like a hurt boy. "You present a problem to me, Callaghan," he said finally, now like a wounded father. "You present the whole problem of the university man."

Dumfounded, I went to tell him again he was wrong. Yet look how worried he was. Since it was a fact he had been good to me, I listened attentively. He, being a varsity graduate himself, wanted to have other university men on the paper, he explained. In the beginning he had been sure I was one who was cut out for newspaper work. Why then did I resist the discipline? Why should a university man grow resentful if told to toe the line? Caught off balance by his troubled honest tone, I was overwhelmed. Me, embodying the problem of the university man! "Tell me," he went on in a kindly tone, "do you smoke too much?" No. Then did I run around with girls and not get enough sleep? As I assured him I had the most temperate habits, I had a grudging respect for his insight. Now at his fatherly best, he was shrewd enough to see that something was going on in me. Paris? Joyce? Pound? My friend Hemingway? No. How could any of this enter his head? I was supposed to be feeling belittled, exiled in the courts. I assured him that from now on I would call out cheerfully, "Good morning, Mr. Hindmarsh," and not spoil his day.

If I would only put my nose to the grindstone I would be a good reporter, he had said, but I could have told him he was wrong about this too. On two or three occasions I had known I wasn't cut out to be a hardboiled old-fashioned reporter. Little things had happened that put me off. A fire at a Muskoka resort hotel took the lives of many guests. All the *Star* men who could be mustered had been taken north on a special train. We had come back and worked all night sorting out the names of those who had been saved and those who had died. Having handed in my story, I found myself standing at the city desk beside my Mr. Johnston, who had in front of him a list of names of those who had died. The telephone kept ringing. I answered, and a woman, giving me her name, asked if there was any word about her daughter. Harry Johnston, running his finger down the list, came to the girl's name among the dead, and whispered to me to tell the mother we had no word that her daughter had died, so could she let us have the girl's picture? The poor mother sounded immensely relieved. She would look for a picture; certainly we could send for it. I hated myself.

On another occasion I was sent to Lake Simcoe to cover a drowning. A storm, coming up suddenly on the lake, had overturned a boy's canoe. All night long a search had been conducted for the boy's body. Late that night I had gone to the cottage of the boy's mother. The weeping woman could hardly hear me asking her for a picture of her son. Like so many other people, the distracted woman seemed to believe that she was under some obligation to the rapacious press. "Oh please," she begged me, "if I could just be left alone," and I knew I had no dignity and her grief had no dignity if I insisted she keep on looking around the cottage for a picture of her drowned boy. The silly front page! The unreality of its importance tormented me. I told her not to be concerned about the picture; just promise not to let any other newpaperman bother her. She promised. I went away. But the next day, of course, a photograph of the drowned boy appeared in the rival newspaper, the *Telegram*.

My sense of reality was often being offended, I say, and besides, with the summer passing, I was having more preposterously comical quarrels with Mr. Hindmarsh. Honestly, I tried to be subdued and respectful to him. Yet whenever he growled at me as he growled at others too, my lip must have curled. We had a showdown over a strange disaster in our town. In a heavy fog a lake boat, bound for the harbor, had crashed into the breakwater two miles away. In the morning I was sent down to the harbor to see the harbor master, a nice man who showed me a map of the harbor and the lakefront. Moving red pins around on the map, he indicated where the ship should have been and how far it had got off its course. Back in the office I wrote the interview which came on the street at noon. An hour later a note was put in my box; it was a note to Mr. Hindmarsh from Joseph Atkinson, the owner; it was a very curt note. The harbor master, a friend of Mr. Atkinson's, had assured Mr. Atkinson it was the duty of a commission, which would be appointed, to determine whether the ship had been off its course. He, the harbor master, would not be so presumptuous as to make such a decision himself. He asked for a retraction and an apology.

White-faced, I hurried into Mr. Hindmarsh's office. "An apology in this case is ridiculous, Mr. Hindmarsh," I said. Jerking back in his chair he glared at me. "Don't you tell me what is ridiculous," he said furiously. "The harbor master insists that he said no such thing to you."

Looking back on it now, I wonder if he wasn't furious because he hated to have to print a ridiculous retraction. Where was the ship if it wasn't off its course? I went on belligerently. That harbor master was calling me a liar. Did he think I made up the story? In his own grim sullen style Hindmarsh repeated that the harbor master denied to Mr. Atkinson that he had made such a statement. That was all there was to it. Oh, no, not on your life, it certainly wasn't all there was to it, I said angrily. We'd see. I rushed out.

"Come back here," he yelled. "What do you think you're going to do?"

"I'm going right down to that man's office. I'll tell him how he moved those pins around—"

"You'll do no such thing," he roared, and he jumped up, slapping both his big palms down on his desk. "You'll do what you're told, do you hear? Now you think you're running this paper." When I said, "You're wrong, Mr. Hindmarsh," his face got so red I thought he would burst a blood vessel.

"Again you tell me I'm wrong. In my own office you keep telling me I'm wrong. Get out of this office. You're fired!"

What do you do when you're fired from a job? Go down to the cashier or work out the week? In the morning I came in to see if my name was on the assignment book. Yes, there it was. Evidently one departed when one picked up one's salary envelope. But on payday, when I opened my envelope, it held no formal dismissal notice, just my salary. Again I was in a quandry. Next morning I kept out of sight, then sneaked a look at the assignment book. My name was there again. So Mr. Hindmarsh, too, was ignoring the fact that I was fired. Good.

But I began to wish fervently I would hear some encouraging news from Paris. What had happened to all my stories? What could Hemingway be doing with them? I wondered. What I overlooked was that my friend, at that time, was fighting desperately for recognition himself. In my mind he might be a big figure in modern literature, but in America he had won the approval of only a small coterie. His beautiful book of stories, *In Our Time,* had been a commercial failure. Deciding to take some action myself, I sent my story, "The Wedding Dress," the story Hemingway had said Tolstoy couldn't have done any better, to *Harper's* Magazine. It bounced back fast without even a word of comment. Either the editor didn't know about Tolstoy or couldn't read, I thought. If I was ever to receive any good news about my work, I seemed to know that it had to come from Paris.

It did not seem to be comical that I was not thinking of France as the place where I might go to cultivate my mind, become aware of the currents of French literature, see Gide, talk to Cocteau, sneer at the naughty boys, Breton and Aragon, expose myself to the marvelously quick French intelligence. No, I thought of Paris as some kind of magical milieu where there would be a vast number of nameless perceptive men who would appreciate my own stories. In the meantime, rather than go on dueling with the ineffable Mr. Hindmarsh, I would study law and pray that within the three years needed for the law course I might get established as a writer. Others had done it by the time they were twenty-five. Scott Fitzgerald had done it.

Remembering how I had talked to Hemingway about Fitzgerald, I wondered if they were now friends. I would find myself looking again at Fitzgerald's early books, *This Side of Paradise* and *The Beautiful and Damned*. The elegant men and girls in these books did not seem to belong to my generation. What did it matter? Fitzgerald had had his own strong talent, as I was sure I had had mine; and in his case an editor, one editor, then the world had suddenly reached out for him. I looked at many pictures of Fitzgerald and I read about his beautiful Zelda. I brought him into my own Toronto world. I couldn't imagine he would like my work, but his early success was always in the back of my mind, giving me faith and hope that soon there would be great news from Paris.

CHAPTER V

I was articled to a plump and amiable young lawyer named Joseph Sedgwick who was just getting established. I used to go to morning law classes and often doze in my chair—the law came easily to me—and then I would go to the law office. If Joe Sedgwick wanted a title searched I did it for him. Otherwise, with him out on business, I would sit in his office at my typewriter working on a short novel. And wasn't I businesslike? As soon as I had finished a chapter I would hand it to the secretary, who would type it promptly and cheerfully just to have something to do. In the office even the few clients wanted to hang around and talk, so there was always a lot of laughter and clowning, and Joe, my lawyer, in his amiable chuckling style, would try to tell me about Dickens as I in turn tried to tell him about Dostoevski.

Having finished my short novel and sent it off to Paris, I

suddenly found myself reading Hemingway's *The Torrents of Spring*. It was a painful experience. How torn I was in my loyalties. My only reader, the only one who believed in me, was satirizing Sherwood Anderson, who, when I was in high school, had brought the world so close. Anderson's style, God knows, had become more affected. Certainly he was vulnerable to mockery and satire, but the mockery shouldn't have come from Hemingway. Why did he do it? But wasn't he also mocking Ford Madox Ford's style? This puzzled me too. Didn't friendship count? And one's own origins? For my part I wanted everybody to know I was grateful to Anderson. Someday I would tell it to him, I knew, and I did too, though I had to wait ten years. Yes, I also remember wishing that it had been at the time I had read *The Torrents of Spring*—not ten years later.

It was at a big cocktail party in Greenwich Village to which I had gone with Bennett Cerf. The apartment was crowded with well-known writers and reviewers, and after an hour of it I, like all the others, was seeking a little attention. Each new face offered the promise of gratifying recognition. Then I saw that my colleagues were all as self-centered and hopeful as I was. Wryly amused and a little ashamed, I withdrew and stood off by myself, looking out the window. In the hum of voices an older man, probably as restless and bored as I, had left his group and came saunter-ing aimlessly in my direction. A square-built man with rugged features and a lion's head. No other man in the world could have looked so much like the pictures of Anderson. All the delight I had got from his work when I had been only nineteen came back to me. Full of affection for this man I had never seen before, I played the clown and did it well. Approaching him with a solemn accusing air, I took him by the arm. "Excuse me, aren't you Sherwood Anderson?" I asked accusingly.

"That's right," he said.

"Good," I said quietly. "Then you're my father."

The look on his face as he drew back uneasily made me want to laugh. I was young enough to be his son. Wild thoughts must have been in his head as he saw the look of recognition on my face. Finally he said, "I don't understand. What is your name?"

"Morley Callaghan."

"Morley . . ." and then he burst out laughing. Delighted, he put his arms around me. "What a wonderful thing to say to me," he said. After we had laughed and shaken hands again, and stood back looking at each other, he said earnestly, "Don't make a mistake about it. You would have written the way you write if you had never heard of me." He was staying at the Washington Mews, he said, insisting I come for dinner next night.

But those years ago in Toronto, reading *The Torrents of Spring*, I couldn't understand why Ernest had felt compelled to kill off old Sherwood. To a man of Ernest's temperament, was it an intolerable frustration to be so definitely linked to Anderson; did he have to kill or reject, or show his superiority in order to be free himself? A man couldn't believe these things about a friend who had been kind and incredibly generous in his interest, and as if to bear out my loyal view of Ernest as a generous man there came suddenly the letter from Paris.

Ernest wrote that his affairs had been unsettled, but now everything had straightened out and he was working rapidly on a novel, writing three thousand words a day. (The novel was *The Sun Also Rises*.) He had carried my stories and my short novel around in his trunk, he wrote. Now he thought he should hand over all my work to Robert McAlmon, of the Contact Press, in Paris, and I would soon be hearing from McAlmon. Well, I only had to wait a week or so.

Since the Contact Press had been Ernest's first publisher, I thought McAlmon and Ernest would be close friends. And that hand-printed edition of *In Our Time* had been dedicated to Robert McAlmon, along with William Bird, and Captain Eric Dormen Smith. Robert McAlmon, publisher of the city of Paris! How sedately impressive it had looked on the Dedication page! In his letter, the first of so many I was to receive from him, McAlmon wrote that my stories had "the odor and timbre of authenticity." What a grand phrase it was! All puffed up, I wanted to look down my nose at someone. Then he compared my stories with the stories Hemingway had done up to that time. What he distrusted in Hemingway's stories, he wrote, was "the hardening process." But in my case the hardening process wasn't there, he wrote. Then he told me he was showing my stories to Ezra Pound and to the editors of *This Quarter* and *transition*. As for my short novel, the Contact Press would do it if I couldn't get a New York publisher. Again I was left waiting for news from Paris.

One winter afternoon at twilight when I was in the law office, I phoned home to ask if there was any mail for me. My mother told me a parcel from Paris was there, and I asked her to open it. In a moment she said, "It's a book or a magazine, and it's called, *This Quarter*." And then I heard her gasp, "Son, your name is on the cover!" I hurried home.

That orange-colored cover of the second number of *This Quarter* had the names of the contributors in bold black lettering: James Joyce, Ezra Pound, Gertrude Stein, Ernest

Hemingway, Emmanuel Carnevali, Kay Boyle, Morley Callaghan. . . . My hands trembling, I opened the magazine and there was my story, "A Girl With Ambition." After dinner I hurried out to meet Loretto. I think we talked for hours. My confidence had become tremendous.

Within a few months my "Last Spring They Came Over" appeared in the second number of *transition*, which was edited by Eugene Jolas and Eliot Paul, and McAlmon wrote me that Ezra Pound would be publishing a magazine of his own in Rapallo, Italy, to be called *The Exile*. Every few weeks now a letter came from McAlmon. And Yvor Winters began to write to me from Palo Alto, California. I remember that in one letter he lectured to me about the danger of becoming, as he called it, "a knickknack for the mantelpiece," and advised me to read Racine. In my native city, of course, the little magazines of Paris had small importance. To my friends, I was still a lazy student at law who went to all the boxing matches and was always seen at the football games. But close at hand were friends of my friends in Paris. In New York were friends of McAlmon, who had lived in the Quarter. So that fall I took a four-day trip to New York to see these friends and hear news of Paris.

I was twenty-two, and I remember that I had my return ticket on the train and fifty dollars. I remember too how I went by way of the Lehigh Valley, and how I came out of the Pennsylvania Station and looked up at the skyscrapers against the sky while my heart leaped. A cop told me where Broadway was. Near Times Square would be the kind of hotel I wanted. On Broadway I began to walk in the wrong direction. An hour later I found myself wandering around Wall Street, so I started to walk uptown again, taking my time, looking around carefully. Near Times Square I found a cheap hotel. My heels were so blistered I had to bathe my feet before I could go out and walk down Fifth and make my first call on Josephine Herbst and John Herrman.

Years later Josephine Herbst would laugh as she told of the way I walked in on her. I still don't know why she laughed. Climbing a long staircase, I knocked and a woman with a good honest face reminding me a little of Lillian Gish's face opened the door.

In the room with the windows overlooking Fifth was a pretty, fair girl with bandaged wrists: the Follies girl, I found out later, who had just tried to commit suicide, and of whom Edmund Wilson had written in *I Thought of Daisy*. I was a friend of Hemingway's and McAlmon's, I said. Maybe I was just too straightforward and candid, I don't know, but I remember that as we talked about McAlmon and Hemingway, and life in Montparnasse, Miss Herbst's fine blue eyes had a grave and sometimes troubled expression. "What's the news from Paris?" she asked. Well, I had it, didn't I? I could give her McAlmon's latest opinion on the literary situation, I could tell her Hemingway had been writing freely and happily at the rate of three thousand words a day, yet I seemed to be making some mistakes. How long since I had been in Paris? she asked. I confessed I had never been in Paris, that I had written my stories in Toronto and that Hemingway had carried them around with him. It was getting darker out and the light in the room had faded, but I kept them there talking to me about Paris. The girl with the bandaged wrists remained motionless and quiet, and I forgot she was there. I could tell Miss Herbst had some kind of generosity of spirit or heart while having a grim hard mind. And I liked her. The room was now in twilight and Miss Herbst said she had an engagement, but I wanted to keep her talking about Paris. She and her husband, John Herrman, could see me the following night, she said. And who else had McAlmon asked me to see? Whipping out my list I asked what kind of a guy Nathan Asch was. Nathan, the son of the great Jewish novelist, Sholem Asch, had just written a book called *The Office*. An amusing talented man who was a little wistful, she said. She told me how to find his street in the Village.

I left, ate in another cafeteria, read the newspapers and sat for an hour, then walked down to Washington Square. The old neighborhood, looking so friendly with all the lights on, filled me with a sense of elation and expectancy. On Bank Street, I think it was, I climbed a stair and knocked on the door and there he was, the young friend of Ford Madox Ford, not long from Paris, with his mustache and thick hair and melancholy eyes. Behind him, stretched out on a bed, was a fair girl, his wife. As I looked around the room and saw that they had no money, I told him McAlmon had asked me to look him up. "What's the news from Paris?" he asked. Again I was the ambassador from Paris. Six months later Nathan told me I had come walking in on them "with all the confidence of a plumber come to fix a pipe." Naturally he had thought I was from Paris. Soon we were talking eagerly about Ford and McAlmon and Hemingway and corners in Montparnasse. Finally I explained I was from Toronto. The confession seemed to charm Nathan, and he told me that if I had as little as five dollars we could see some of the Village spots, having only coffee at one place, then coffee again at another. We went out happily. What a happy night it was. The whole three days were a delight.

I met Josephine Herbst's husband, John Herrman, a tall handsome laughing man. Part of each day I spent with

Nathan Asch. We all treated each other as important writers. And one evening I went out to Rutherford and had dinner with Dr. William Carlos Williams and his wife. Everyone was so friendly, and all because I had had a few stories in the Paris magazines. No wonder I was back in New York within six months. The places, the faces, are all a little blurred now; a rap on a roominghouse door, Allen Tate, the poet with the scholarly head opening the door; a big party in some kind of a loft with Eddie Cahill suffering from some kind of stomach trouble; sitting beside Katherine Anne Porter at a dinner, wondering why she went home alone; the party where I met Ford Madox Ford and was baffled, wondering why I couldn't approach him eagerly, but he seemed too impassive, too roundly, solidly imposing with his walrus mustache as he presided port-winedly over the gathering, talking in a hoarse whisper that compelled everyone to lean forward, alert and attentive, to catch the whispered words—he had been gassed in the war, you know. How secretly enchanted I was by the experience of being with people who regarded writing as more important than anything else on earth. But, of course, I was the only one who hadn't been to Europe.

CHAPTER VI

Though as yet a great way off, some of the malice and resentments born of broken friendships in Paris began to reach me. Robert McAlmon, Hemingway's first publisher, wrote to me about *The Sun Also Rises,* which had come out and made Hemingway fashionable and famous, that he would feel more confident of Hemingway's talent if he hadn't turned to the rich pastures of Michael Arlen. Wasn't Lady Brett right out of the same bag as Arlen's Iris March in *The Green Hat?* In other letters he would tell me of annoying aspects of Hemingway's personality; he would concentrate usually on something he had seen going on between Hemingway and his wife. And as for Hemingway himself, why was he always hardening himself up? The answer was obvious. Anyone close to him knew he was really soft and sentimental. It was amusing to remember the Hemingway who had first come to Montparnasse. Ask anybody. Why had he been wearing those three heavy sweaters to make himself look husky and powerful? What a ridiculous give-away.

I used to read these letters and brood over them at night by myself in a little lending library I had opened. My young newspaper friend, Art Kent, had conned me into opening this library with him on the theory that we could have a woman run it, and get a little weekly income for ourselves. When Art couldn't raise his share of the money I stupidly and stubbornly kept on with the library, which was costing me money, using the place as a night headquarters and writing my stories there while waiting for Loretto to join me. Well, these letters I read so carefully told me that McAlmon, who had helped Hemingway, had turned against him. Now he could hardly hide his malice. What went on among old friends in Paris? I used to wonder. Anderson and Hemingway. Hemingway, too, had turned against Ford. Why was McAlmon now making sure that I had his own mocking view of my friend? How could he assume that I was soon to meet Hemingway again? How could he be so sure? It was mysterious. Then I would say to myself, "Supposing Hemingway was only interested in my work? Supposing he doesn't think of himself as my friend?" Such thoughts were foolish. As it was I saw no immediate prospect of walking in on him.

But people with Paris connections began to walk in on me. One day a shy, prematurely balding man with a bad stutter, named Raymond Knister, came into the bookstore. A countryman of mine who had actually written in *This Quarter!* He told me he had worked in Chicago on a little magazine called *The Midland*. Unbelievably, he knew what was going on in literature in Paris, London and New York. Immediately I wrote to Hemingway, calling attention to Knister's farm poetry in *This Quarter*. And immediately Hemingway answered—but didn't mention the poetry. This Raymond Knister was a strange man. Sometimes I wanted to punch him on the nose. He had a kind of suspiciousness I couldn't cope with. Having told me that he had never been paid any money for his poems in *This Quarter*, he then decided that the editor could have sent the small check to me to pass on to him. I would snarl bitterly, "For God's sake, why don't you write to them and ask them about it?" But he would only smile knowingly. It was a fantastic summer anyway. As I say, everyone and everything began to come my way. In the beginning Nathan Asch came up from New York to see me, stayed a month, and in the evenings in the library we used to play a game of handball, a point being scored every time the ball bounced directly against the edge of a shelf. And when Nathan had gone I heard from Ezra Pound, who was in Rapallo, Italy. Two stories of mine, "A Predicament" and "Ancient Lineage" were to appear in the one issue of his *Exile*. While I was walking around in a trance, rejoicing that Ezra Pound admired my work, I heard that Max Perkins at Scribner's, having read a story of mine called "Amuck in the Bush" in the *American Caravan*, and having then asked to see more stories, had also got hold of the one Ezra Pound had ("A Predicament") and wanted another one. I quickly sent it to him. Then Perkins asked if I could get Pound to release "The Predicament" to them. I cabled Pound. Wondering how everything had happened so swiftly, wondering, too, if Hemingway had spoken to Perkins, I set out for New York to see Perkins.

CHAPTER VII

It was late in the winter, maybe just approaching spring, for I remember I had my heavy coat on, standing on Fifth Avenue at 48th, looking up at Scribner's publishing house. I was to have lunch with the famous editor, the friend of Fitzgerald and Hemingway. Not nervous at all, just expectant and rather wary, I entered the building. I asked the elevator man for Mr. Perkins' office, then a girl showed me where the office was. At the door a tall sandy-haired, or sandy-complexioned, man with a thin proud face, smiling faintly, put out his hand to me. Since he had his hat on I thought we were going right out. But he asked me to take off my coat. Should I too leave my hat on? I wondered. Max Perkins didn't seem to be the alert and lively businessman I had imagined. Yet there was something about him that was familiar; it was as if I had met him at university, and he

seemed to fumble around for words, withdraw into himself
a little, his eyes not on mine, saying one thing, then words
belonging to another thought suddenly coming at me from
another angle. Often he would be looking out the window,
leaving me alone and waiting. It struck me, watching him,
that maybe he wore his hat in the office and maybe went
hatless outside. Wary as I was, I knew immediately I could
trust him. While apparently fumbling around rather awkwardly with his words he was getting some kind of a sharp
impression of me. All right, there I was, let him go ahead.

Then he said, looking puzzled and exasperated, "We heard
from your friend Ezra Pound." He heaped it all right on me.
Pound had written a violently abusive letter when giving
them permission to use my story. The fact that they had
published Hemingway and now were interested in me,
Pound wrote, didn't excuse them for the years they had
spent publishing worthless junk. The letter had been full of
abuse. Pound had berated them for all the sins of the whole
New York publishing world. Inwardly I groaned. Why the
hell would Ezra Pound bother doing it? Why should he want
to insult them when he knows they're now interested in
me? There was Perkins, looking puzzled and aggrieved, and
I thought he was holding Pound's abuse against me. I tried
to laugh. I tried to explain that Ezra Pound had such a
hatred of standard smooth mediocrity and such indignation
against publishers for refusing to recognize authentic writers,
he was simply taking out his anger on Scribner's, because
they at least had proven they were aware of authentic work.
Maybe Pound had decided there was no use berating other
publishers; they wouldn't even know what he was talking
about. Besides, he himself had been ignored for years in
New York. No man in the world, though, was a better judge

of good writing. But how could I know he would write such a letter?

No, no, no, he wasn't holding it against me, Perkins said, getting his coat. He was merely trying to understand Ezra Pound. As we went out my confidence was shaken, for Perkins had made it clear that I had an abusive champion whose temperament was past his understanding. We went around the corner to Cheerio's, the restaurant where Perkins always ate.

Even in the restaurant, checking our coats, it seemed to me that Perkins was reluctant to give his hat to the girl. And this strange man, whom I had immediately liked, wouldn't give me a chance to talk about writing. While we were eating he kept asking me idle little questions about myself, my background, the university, my girl. In his random, entirely inoffensive fashion he was like a skilled insurance investigator. Sometimes I wanted to shriek, "What about my works? Never mind my school, my legal training, my view of a gentleman." Suddenly he mentioned the success they had had with *The Sun Also Rises;* it had looked for a month as if the book wouldn't catch on; the sale had started in a Wall Street bookstore. It gave me a chance to tell him Hemingway had been my only reader and booster. I assumed, I said, that Hemingway had told him about me. No, he said in surprise. He wasn't aware that I knew Hemingway. It had been Scott Fitzgerald who had talked most enthusiastically to him about my work, and I'm sure then my eyes went blank with astonishment. Fitzgerald, not Hemingway! Yes, Fitzgerald had been in New York, he said, at the time when he, Perkins, had read my story in the *American Caravan.* Fitzgerald, quickly taking up my case, had gone back to his hotel, got a copy of one of the Paris magazines which had a story of mine in it and brought it back to Perkins. Fitzgerald had been enthusiastic, excited about the story. Fitzgerald? I couldn't believe it.

Though we then talked about my novel *Strange Fugitive*, which Scribner's had, we finished lunch without Perkins having revealed at all whether he had any plans for me. Never had I felt so at loose ends as when we left the restaurant, then turned the corner on Fifth. We had been talking about Princeton men. Scribner's seemed to like Princeton men. Then, almost as if it had slipped his mind, Perkins said Scribner's would publish my novel, and then in the following season they would also like to do a book of short stories. The trouble was the thing had been so underplayed that the news, offered so quickly and quietly there on the street in the sunlight, made me feel obliged as a gentleman to underplay my satisfaction. Anyone watching would have believed that two men coming up the street were talking about something as trivial as the weather. We went back into Scribner's, had a little talk about Scribner contracts, and we shook hands. For the first time I noticed a gentle warm approval in his smile.

Only when I had got outside did I feel that something of vast and mysterious significance had happened. I said to myself, "I have a publisher! Two books of mine are coming out!" And it seemed to me that a lot of people should be gathering around me on the sunlit street. Turning, I looked up Fifth Avenue, watching the way the tall buildings sloping up in the sunlight went reaching into the blue sky. It was the most beautiful street in the world. Slowly, I walked down the street, slowly, vaguely, yet my whole body felt light. To this day whenever I am on Fifth Avenue I feel good. But somebody had to hear the news, someone very close to me. I couldn't reach Loretto. I went into a telegraph office and wired my mother and father: SCRIBNER'S TOOK TWO BOOKS. Back on Fifth again, looking around, I thought of those lines of Balzac's Rastignac: "Oh, to be famous and loved." Well, I was sure of my girl, sure I would soon be famous.

Then I remember thinking suddenly of Scott Fitzgerald going into Scribner's with my story. Of all people—Fitzgerald! Fitzgerald who had been in my mind so vividly some months ago! The talks I had about him with Loretto! The discussions of his work I had with Hemingway in the beginning. The whole world suddenly seemed to contract, become so small I had only to think of someone and he was suddenly in my life. Whom I was to meet, what was to happen to me, seemed beyond my control. As for Fitzgerald's own work, the characters of his early novels seemed to be out of my time. But with *The Great Gatsby* he had become another kind of an artist, in beautiful control of his material and all his effects, wonderfully suggestive, too, bringing the people in his story close to my own life. I wanted to meet him, seemed to know instinctively I would feel happy and close to him. Turning suddenly, I walked up the Avenue in the sunlight as far as the park, then I crossed over to the little square and the fountain by the Plaza. No one was sitting on the benches. It was too cold. The park looked bleak in the sunlight. Looking at the Plaza I could think of Fitzgerald. Entering by the side door, I walked slowly through the marble halls, past the desk and out through the 57th Street entrance. To this day whenever I pass the Plaza, Scott comes into my head. Years later, well, just last year, waiting in there for my publisher, Jack

Geoghegan, who had got caught in crosstown traffic, I found myself thinking of Scott again.

That night, on the way home on the train, I remembered that Perkins had said Fitzgerald was in Paris. Soon I, too, would be there. It was a settled matter now. However, the obligation to my parents made it necessary for me to finish law school, but then—with a little luck—well, we would see what happened when my books came out. Nor did I have long to wait. In a few months *Scribner's* Magazine had appeared with two of my stories in the one issue, a big green band around the magazine heralding a new fiction star. The *New Yorker* wrote, asking for a story. When my novel *Strange Fugitive* appeared, it got considerable attention. I waited anxiously to hear from Hemingway. Finally the letter came. I was having some luck and he was glad, he wrote, and then he explained why he himself hadn't gone to Scribner's with my stories. He had seen that I was going good, turning out many stories, all good, and he knew that quick publication could upset a writer. The main thing was to have nothing happen to upset a writer when the stories were all coming out right for him. Brooding over his letter, I saw there was wisdom in his point of view. No man had more wisdom about handling his talent. Later, I heard he had said I had become a professional writer too young. I smiled to myself.

When I went again to New York at the time *Strange Fugitive* came out, the business manager at Scribner's, Whitney Darrow, who took me out to dinner, told me with enthusiasm that in their promotion of my novel they had tied me up with Hemingway. A success with *The Sun Also Rises?* All right, tie me in with that success, you understand? Oh, they certainly did! And the mill run of reviewers picked up the cue.

Later, when I left Scribner's for good, Max Perkins told me earnestly there was one thing he wanted me to know: it had never been his idea to associate me and my work with Hemingway. From the beginning he had seen that I had entirely different perceptions.

But at the time of my launching I was bewildered and hurt. I could see I might be ruined. For some years Hemingway had been my only writer friend and reader. Now suddenly the reviewers were hitting me on the head in Hemingway's name. Nor could I expect Hemingway to send up smoke signals explaining that three years ago he had read as many of my stories as I had of his. Yet I knew it couldn't embarrass me, meeting Ernest as meet him now I surely would.

But in a letter to a mutual friend, he had made one critical comment that puzzled me about a story of mine—a story about a prizefighter—that had appeared in *Scribner's* Magazine. And he told this friend that when Morley wrote stories about the things he knew, there was no one any better, but he should stick to the things he knew something about. What was bothering Ernest? I wondered. Did he think that in writing about a fighter I had made an unworthy excursion into his own imaginary world? Was it because I had forgotten to tell him I had done a lot of boxing and went to all the fights? Well, what did it matter? The main thing was I would soon see him. . . .

Having graduated from law school I married Loretto. The night before our marriage, the April night before we left for Paris, I went boxing with my best man, Joe Mahon, a college friend, a heavyweight, now a lawyer, who had won the international intercollegiate heavyweight championship at West Point. I was no match for him, if he put on any real pressure, but we had been boxing two or three times a week, and as he said, I was very fast with my hands. That night, sparring, circling around the big fellow, I noticed a grim smile on his face. He kept jabbing at my eyes. It tickled his sense of humor to think of me showing up at my wedding with a black eye. Just before we quit, he, in his eagerness and frustration, swung so hard to my head that when he missed, for the first time in all our boxing he fell flat on his face, and I danced around laughing.

CHAPTER VIII

On the way to Paris we stopped over in New York and had lunch with Perkins, and I had to smile to myself watching him draw out my wife, making sure she belonged, just as he had done with me. When he learned that she had gone to a convent he seemed pleased. With surprising firmness he said all girls ought to be educated in convents. What about his five daughters? I wondered. With his soft approach, sometimes appearing to be intellectually way out in left field, what a firm-minded man he was. So firm in his opinions about women, too, with certain fatalistic convictions: a man wouldn't stay married to a woman older than he was, it couldn't last; a woman could be bad for a writer; a woman could be— Well, I got the impression that women who plunged into a man's world were a nuisance.

And he had a baffling superiority. A neighbor of Perkins'

in New Caanan, also a friend of mine, told me that he often sat beside Perkins on the train and could never get him into a conversation. He said to Perkins once, "I think Morley has a chance of becoming another Galsworthy," and Perkins, looking at him coldly, said, "Galsworthy! That third-rater," and went on reading his paper. My broker friend said to me, "What is this? Galsworthy is Scribners' best-selling author!" And, I, talking to Perkins about the same broker, said once, "I think he might help me to make some money." Perkins said rudely, "Tell him to buy one of your books and let it go at that." An impossible man, the broker had said, and yet I trusted Perkins completely. He had an ethic, not a hand-to-mouth ethic, a truly aristocratic ethic I felt at home with.

At lunch that day I could see my wife felt at home with him, too. He had just read the manuscript of *A Farewell to Arms*, and he talked about it, his head on one side, a little smile on his face. Some people would say it was a very sentimental book, he said. And indeed it was sentimental. But it was good sentiment, and there was the splendid contrast of the beautiful countryside against the ugliness of war. Then he began to grumble about Americans who went to Paris to become expatriated. It was all wrong, and he hoped we wouldn't stay too long in Paris. Just the same we were to be sure to look up Scott Fitzgerald. Here was his address. But shouldn't he give us a letter of introduction? No, it would be ridiculous. Nothing as formal as that was needed. Just walk in on Scott and he would be delighted. Were Ernest and Scott good friends? Indeed they were, Perkins said to my delight. Scott had some kind of a warm boyish personal admiration for Ernest; Ernest was so physically active, capable of such extraordinary exploits. And then, his head on one side, a little wondering smile on his face, Perkins told me he had heard that Ernest, in some French town, had been watching the middleweight champion of France in a bout with some hapless incompetent fighter and the champion, making a monkey out of him, had been punishing him badly. And after the bout had ended, Ernest had jumped into the ring and knocked out the champion. The story sounded incredible to me. I had noted in the beginning in the *Star* newsroom that Ernest had had that fatal capacity for making men want to tell fantastic stories about him. Yet how did I know about this one? Perkins obviously believed it. It stuck in my mind as if I knew I was to hear it again.

One other thing, Perkins said, as we finished lunch. Before we left town we were to see Sinclair Lewis, my great booster. Lewis had just written a front-page article in the *Herald Tribune* about my work. We would go back to the office, Perkins said, and he would telephone Lewis and tell him we were coming to see him.

How lovely New York looked that April afternoon, with the sun shining and the trees on the Village streets all green. On the way to Paris dropping by to see Sinclair Lewis! And he wanted to see us. Imagine!

In those days Lewis had a house in the Village. My wife and I were apprehensive as we knocked on the door. Lewis, who had just written *Dodsworth* and was at the height of his fame, had recently married Dorothy Thompson. I had a feeling Lewis might want to take back all the kind things he had said about me as soon as he saw me. To me he was the author of *Babbitt*, a remarkable book. In all his other work he had a splendid gift for mimicry, a great eye for detail and for what made people pretentious and ridiculous. Yet it seemed to me that his grand success was based on one of his weaknesses as an artist: he gave the reader a chance at too quick a recognition. This kind of writing always puts the writer and the reader in a comfortable relationship, neither one being required to jar himself, or get out of this groove of recognition. A writer who has this gift is always meeting his reader and reviewers on their terms, and it should be always the other way around. But in *Babbitt*, Lewis had gone beyond the mimicry, beyond that area of amused recognition where the reader can share the writer's easy superiority; Babbitt had become a warm living human being.

The door was opened by a grinning, balding man. It was Lou, the secretary, the Lewis man. In the drawing room a writer, Mary Heaton Vorse, sat talking to Lewis, who looked almost frighteningly like a picture I had seen of him. A gaunt thin sandy man, with staring protuberant blue eyes, many freckles on his flushed face; the forehead broad, the face tapering sharply—skin over a skull. This strange excited wild face lit up as he came to me with his arms out. "Well, well, well," he cried, pushing me back a little. "Let me get a good look at you." And then, laughing, he looked at my wife. "You're charming," he said to her. "Just right for him." He sent the grinning Lou scurrying for drinks. All the time we were there Lou kept on grinning. "Do you know, Morley," Lewis said earnestly, "Flaubert would have loved your work. Yes, old Flaubert."

His approach, his appraisal, were so candid, his pale blue eyes still so full on me, I couldn't get my bearings. I was a young man who liked to play things down. I told him I should have thanked him for writing about me. No, no, no, he insisted fervently. Never make that mistake. Such thanks were an insult to a man's critical intelligence. What was a critic's sole distinction? His ability to recognize something new and good. Take away that flash of perception and he had nothing. If you patted him on the back you made him feel he was much brighter than he usually was, and in that case he ought to feel insulted. Wasn't that right? As the words poured out of him happily, we weren't exactly exchanging opinions. I could hardly get a word in edgewise. Mary Heaton Vorse could do little but smile approvingly. Then he would pause for breath, his head on one side, shake his head, chuckle and regard me. "Just like his work, isn't he?" So we were going to Paris? Well, he could give us letters of introduction. He had friends in London, Paris, Rome.

Then suddenly his manner changed, that light in his eyes changed too, and though his tone was aggressive, almost magically he became defensive. It was not likely, the way I wrote, that I would be called a journalist. Someday, though, someone might say it of me. Don't ever let it bother me. His startling blue eyes, now troubled, on me, he said, "They call me a journalist, you know. Well, H. G. Wells told me once that they called him a journalist, too, and he said, 'Don't ever let it trouble you that they called you a journalist.'" Then there was a solemn silence. The gaiety all gone, he sat brooding, and I too. And in the silence, I, the young writer, caught a glimpse of some gnawing discontent in this enormously successful novelist. When I grew older was I to know this discontent? I wondered. What was he communicating to me? Then, suddenly, he looked up as if aware he was out of character. If we had been alone and drinking he might have told me about his lonely life as a writer; the way he wanted to be seen; the way others actually saw him. Then the spell, the desire to be in comfortable protective character, was again on him. "No matter," he said, trying to recover the now slightly spurious gusto. How was my book doing? How was it received?

In the current issue of the *Saturday Review of Literature* there had been a review, I said. It had annoyed me. Not that it wasn't a good review, but the tone was annoying. "Lou," he called. "Bring me the *Saturday Review*," and Lou, grinning happily as if from long experience he knew it was all part of a joke, scurried around looking for the magazine. "Yes, this is a good review," Lewis said, as he read. "The man meant well. It is sympathetic." And then his face lit up magically. "Ah, I see what you mean," he said. The reviewer had said my characters were the kind of people you meet straphanging on subways.

And now he became like an elf, an imp, looking like one, too, with his strange compelling face, dancing around in an antic light. "Lou," he called, "get me Henry Seidel Canby." When I protested nervously there was no point in calling the editor of the *Saturday Review,* he only laughed. Lou, now, was on the telephone. The tone I objected to was worth objecting to, Lewis said. It should always be objected to. Walking up and down he seemed to be off by himself.

Lou called out that Henry Canby was not at the office. Then he might be in his home in Connecticut, Lewis answered impatiently. Wherever he was, get him. By now we had become merely spectators, watching Lewis as he smiled to himself.

Then Lou called out that Henry Canby had been traced to his home in Connecticut; here he was. With an encouraging smile to us, Lewis picked up the phone, but he kept his eyes on us, his audience.

The dialogue between Lewis and Canby, as I remember it, went something like this: "Henry, I just read that review you've done of Morley Callaghan's stories." A big dancing-eyed grin to us as he listened. Then he answered earnestly,

"Henry, I don't deny it's a good review. The intention is certainly good. But Henry, it's patronizing. Worse, Henry, it represents dreadful snobbery. Listen to these lines, Henry," and then in an aggrieved tone he read the lines about the straphangers on subways. If he hadn't been grinning happily at us I would have sworn that he was a mortally wounded man. "The point is simple, Henry," he went on. "Who are these straphangers? I'm the one who's insulted, Henry. Why? Why shouldn't I be? Do you know, Henry, that I have a brother who is a conductor on a streetcar? Do you know my brother makes fifty dollars a week?"

By the way Lou was chuckling to himself I could tell Lewis didn't have such a brother. "You've insulted my brother, Henry," he went on in his aggrieved, bitter tone. "I can assure you, Henry, my brother's feelings are the same as mine. Just because he's a conductor has he no dignity? Isn't he just as much a human being as I am? Do you know what you're doing, Henry, publishing this review? You're looking down your nose at me and my brother and human beings like us all over America."

By now he was so absorbed in his own performance he seemed to have forgotten about us. Even when he paused to let Canby get a word in, he would shake his head angrily, go to protest, his expression wonderfully stern and aggrieved. Then he seemed to relent a little; the hurt proud man being soothed. In a mollified tone he agreed that the *Saturday Review of Literature* had not deliberately insulted him or his brother, nor had the good citizens all over America any real cause for savage resentment. "All right, Henry, I believe you," he said. "As long as you understand it's important to me." Then Canby, evidently moving in shrewdly, caught him off balance. "No, I can't do it," Lewis said. "I can't write another review. I've just written about the book, Henry, in the *Herald Tribune.*" He had to go on protesting he couldn't have pieces about the same book in two publications. But he would think of someone else who might do it. Adopting a sweet, grateful tone, he thanked Canby for grasping so quickly his concern about his brother's feelings, and hung up. Then he rose and faced us, chuckling and beaming, delighted by our laughter.

Suppose he did love acting, nevertheless, I had the strange feeling that he really wanted to be someone else. And why? Why did he want to mask himself? He was a strange-looking man, but in himself, just being himself, as he had been talking seriously a few moments ago, he was an attractive man.

Sitting down, and serious now, he said Canby would publish another review by anyone he suggested. Don't go on with it, I begged him. Gradually he recovered his pep, his pitch, only now he was pulling us headlong into his own life. What a pity we couldn't stay around and meet Dorothy Thompson, he said. Though we were young enough to be his children, and were strangers to him, he told us how happy he expected to be with Miss Thompson; how his whole life would change, how he had needed such an understanding woman. Our regret that we couldn't meet Miss Thompson was so sincere it pleased him. Jerking his head back, smiling to himself as he regarded me fondly, he said, "Just think. I could put you in the way of making thirty thousand a year right now." I sat up straight, all ears, basking in a dream of incredible opulence. Then he shook his head firmly. "No, it wouldn't be good for you right now, Morley. Go on in your own way."

"I'm afraid I'll have to," I said, sighing.

Before we left he gave us a copy of his new book, *Dodsworth.* He told us we would love Paris. We were to let him know if he could help us.

Outside, my wife and I started to laugh, then fell silent. We were both still bemused. All Lewis' energy, change of mood, goodwill, gaiety, had left us feeling a little drunk. Was the literary life all on this grand, opulent and theatrical scale? But after we had joked and shared our pleasure in Lewis, I remember I wondered with some pain, since I liked and admired him, why he used all his frantic energy in cultivating unreality? Why was he so bent on protecting himself that people might have no chance of judging his worth as a human being? I think he was really a shy man being afraid of his own shyness, his own natural warmth and generosity; he clowned his way out of his loneliness.

We were staying at the old Brevoort on lower Fifth. In the morning, letters of introduction came from Lewis, and a note saying he had sent his man, Lou, to St. Patrick's Cathedral to light candles for our safe journey to Paris.

CHAPTER IX

Lonely men who are always in public places, men like Sinclair Lewis, have always interested me. Perhaps they are able to sense that I am drawn to them, for I can't remember ever making the first approach. Just as it was part of my writing creed to distrust calculated charm in prose, so as a person, I suppose I felt it was beneath me to try to ingratiate myself with anyone who aroused my curiosity. Yet in one way or another I seem to get around to knowing the isolated men who interest me.

On the ship one night at dinnertime my wife said, "Look at the priest sitting all by himself at the table over there. Why have they stuck him there all by himself?" The reddish-haired, balding, freckle-faced, powerfully built priest didn't look aloof and self-contained; he simply looked like a man left alone in a big dining room. At our table there were five of us; a solid Middle Western businessman and his wife, both pleasant and both dull, and the ship's doctor, an incredibly noble stuffed owl of a man. At the captain's table were at least eight passengers, all in a convivial mood, and among them in jolly splendor, the Anglican or Episcopalian clergyman. Of course, it was an English ship.

After dinner in the lounge my wife spoke to the big lonely priest, and we sat down with him for an hour, and he told us about himself. This priest, whom I'll call Father Tom, for he may still be alive, was the Catholic chaplain for a California penitentiary housing incorrigible criminals who were there for life. In ten years he had walked to the execution chamber with sixteen men. All this year he had been breaking out into strange intermittent fevers. His superiors and the doctors had grown daily more worried about him. They had persuaded him to take a three months' leave of absence, tour the Mediterranean, then visit his old mother in Ireland. Above all, the doctors said, he was to try and enjoy himself; forget the prison, throw all his cares away, and at least for three months try to find some joy in life. He was to join his touring party in Paris.

Yet he was a jolly, jesting, laughing man. He had a quick intelligence. What a relief to be talking to him after listening all through dinner to the endless flow of clichés from the ship's doctor, whose punch line was "Quite, oh, quite," and the solid banalities of the bluff businessman and his goodhearted wife. That night leaving us, the priest told us that he was to say Mass on Sunday on the tourist deck, the Anglican clergyman having been given the care of the souls of the first-class passengers. Would we be sure to come to Mass on Sunday? It was a little thing, but after all, we weren't Anglicans, were we? We assured him we would come.

On deck the next day I spoke to him cheerfully and asked him how he was passing the time. Surprised, he looked at me, laughed, then wanted to talk. He had assumed that our friendship would not go beyond last night's polite encounter. A woman speaks to a priest; her husband listens sympathetically while the priest gropes around trying to tell them something about himself, the husband says little, and the priest asks them to go to Mass because he is a bit piqued at being regarded as an isolated figure among the first-class passengers. It was a pleasure, he said, to find I was a talkative man myself. We certainly talked, and about the philosophy of St. Thomas Aquinas. He was sharp-minded, and began to put me on.

After that, he attached himself to us. Nor did we tire of his company. At one moment he would be talking about the prison inmates; no penitentiary should be built that denied an inmate some wild hope of escape. Not that a convict might necessarily bring himself to try an escape. But he had a right to his harmless dreams, the exercise of all his ingenuity in his dream; it kept his mind alive; the remote possibility represented a last hope for men condemned to life imprisonment. Without this hope in the back of their minds the convicts would go crazy, he contended. Another time he would start talking about the views of St. Thomas on love, or hell as the deprivation of the love of God, or St. Thomas' idea of beauty. Sometimes he would be chuckling to himself, just testing out my knowledge of St. Thomas. Or if we tired of convicts and philosophers he would have me exercise my gift for malice in little descriptions of the other passengers. He had a fine barbed comic spirit himself. Other passengers who might have noticed him at his lonely table would have been astonished by his alert awareness of their pretentions. Yet he would add charitably after some jest about an officer, "He's probably a good soul, a kind man. God forgive us." I had noticed that often he would ask to be excused. Within half an hour he would reappear on deck, his hair freshly combed, his face washed, and wearing a fresh clerical collar. Sometimes, it is true, when he reappeared, he smelled strongly of whiskey. What was the idea? I asked, teasing him. Did he have to change his clothes to take a drink? No, he said apologetically. It was the sweat. Three times a day he would break out into sweats and be soaking wet, and he had to go and change all his clothes. It was also a good time to take a drink, wasn't it? But suddenly I avoided his eyes. I had a hunch that the doctors who had told him to tour the Mediterranean and have a good time had been sure that he had not long to live.

When the ship landed at Le Havre, I remember how he came to us chuckling to himself. Nodding at a portly gentleman who had taken a grandly opulent air with some friends, he said, "See that fellow? He's boasting that he had the biggest bar bill of all the passengers. I dare not disillusion him. But the fact is the steward just told me I did, and promised to keep it a secret."

On the trip to Paris I was so taken up with my own dreams and my sense of satisfaction at coming to the journey's end where I would meet my friends, I didn't pay much attention to the priest. I was reminding Loretto I had told her five years ago I would bring her to Paris. The priest may have been sitting behind us on the train. We didn't realize he wouldn't let us get out of sight. I was excited and eager. Even the neighborhoods of Paris seemed to be known to me.

At college I had studied French. The history of Paris; the heroes, even the pictures of the principal buildings, the churches, the square were in the front of my mind. I couldn't believe I was a stranger. But coming out of the St. Lazare station, asking a porter for directions, I found my French was abominable. I had no sense of direction. Since we had McAlmon's address, the Paris-New York Hotel on the rue Vaugirard, we would get into a taxi and go to this hotel. It was about noontime. Then Father Tom appeared beside us, taking my arm. Like a shy apologetic boy, he asked us if we would have lunch with him at the Café de la Paix. Before he joined his touring party, he said, he would like to sit with us at some famous French café, and he had heard of this one.

For April it was surprisingly chilly, about as chilly as it would have been back home, so we ate inside the café and drank too much wine. Outside on the rue de la Paix the girls were passing, taxis whirled by, the street life of Paris was just beyond our window. And I nursed a sweet satisfaction. For a long time, in my dream, I had seen us sitting here just this way.

The priest was to meet his party at a small Right Bank hotel, and we went with him to this hotel where we decided to register for the night so we could get our bearings. Then the priest had to leave us. "I don't know what it'll be like on this tour," he said gloomily. "Well, look here. I'll be back in June. I could look you up, couldn't I? Would you mind very much?" Then he added in a resigned tone, "Ah, no, you'll forget all about me." We swore we wouldn't, and as we watched him cross the lobby to meet an official of his tour, he had his head back like a man staunchly resigned to the company of a hundred middle-aged women, and convinced he would be allowed to drown in the depth of our memories without leaving a ripple.

While in the hotel I telephoned McAlmon. So many letters had passed between us that when I spoke to him I expected to recognize his voice. Come over to his Left Bank hotel and see him, he said. "Well, here I go," I said to Loretto as I left her, and we knew I was opening the first door, taking a taxi to the Paris-New York on the rue Vaugirard.

CHAPTER X

Surely my expectation of friendship with McAlmon was soundly based, for not only had he got my stories published, he had been willing to publish them himself. My curiosity about this generous man was immense. Of all the Americans who had been in Paris—those who appear in memoirs and movies—McAlmon is the overlooked man. Not only did his Contact Press first publish Hemingway, but it published Gertrude Stein's *The Making of Americans*. And as I found out, he had the friendship of Joyce and Pound as well as William Carlos Williams. He was willing to help any writer of talent. And what did he get for it? Sneers and open hostility. Suppose he did write sloppy prose himself. It was his awareness of what was fresh and new and good in other writers that made him enormously superior to his detractors—the aesthetes. The writers about writers. In his letters to me he had shown himself arrogant and contemptuous, but I didn't hold it against him; it had given his letters an edge, a tang. And I had felt the secret envy of him in some of my friends in New York, for marrying Bryher, the writer, who was the daughter of Sir John Ellerman, the shipping magnate, one of the rich men of England. After bumming his way across America, doing everything from dishwashing to modeling for painters and sculptors in New York, it had been a very nice thing for him to marry a rich girl and get a handsome divorce settlement, but I had always believed his story that he hadn't been aware it was to be a marriage in name only; he had insisted he was willing to be interested in women. And with the money, what did he do? Spend it all on himself? No, he became a publisher, he spent the money on other people he believed in.

In New York I heard this little ditty:

> I'd rather live in Oregon
> And pack salmon,
> Than live in Nice
> And write like Robert McAlmon.

And this little ditty was in my mind when I rapped on his hotel door, and it opened, and at last there he was. "How are you, come on in," McAlmon said laconically. He looked a little like his letters; about thirty-five, sort of nervous and crowded and with restless blue eyes. About my height, he was slim, long-nosed, thin-lipped and handsome, and, of course, he had the arrogant or contemptuous tilt to his head. But his low-toned greeting put me off. Entering the room I seemed to know he had looked at me and been unimpressed. It's hard to meet a man who has helped you from afar and believe you see this look in his eyes. But I didn't understand that if

Tolstoy himself had appeared suddenly in the room, Mc-Almon wouldn't have been impressed. And I can see too, now, that the encounter was a comic checkmating of two temperaments; it had to be casual and laconic. As a young reporter I had acquired an air of being professionally unimpressed. With him the same attitude was a point of honor. And so we faced each other after three years of letter writing as if we had been having a beer every afternoon for years.

Pointing at the packed bag on the bed he explained that in an hour he was leaving for the South of France. To meet me, to part from me so quickly, it was all the same to him, he didn't care, his eyes seemed to say. So I, for my part, didn't sound the slighest bit brokenhearted at the news. How unsentimental we were as we sized each other up, he, hardly looking, and I watching him directly all the time! Sitting down, he looked straight at me for the first time. He began to thaw. He even smiled at me as he talked about the Quarter with a belittling wit that made me laugh. His lip kept twisting in an ironic smile. I began to like him, not as you approvingly like a man, but as if you knew you would have some strange sneaking liking and respect for him no matter how badly he behaved. And that was the way it was always to be between me and McAlmon. Now I wished he wasn't going away. Suppose no one known to me was in Paris and we were left alone?

I asked if Hemingway was in town. It brought McAlmon to life in another way; it was as if he saw that I was counting on meeting another good friend. It upset him and he brooded over it. He and Hemingway didn't see much of each other now, he admitted. With his curling lip, McAlmon could never admit he had been hurt in a friendship; it had to be the other way around; this way: Hemingway had revealed an aspect of his personality that made one look down his nose at him. With a little laugh and a careless wave of his hand, as if it were really all unimportant, he nevertheless began to belittle Ernest. They had gone together to Spain, he drawled. In Spain, he had been the one who had introduced Hemingway to the run of the little bulls at Pamplona. Coming back, at one of the train stops, there had been a corpse rotting in the sun—a dog, an animal of some kind. And Hemingway, contemplating the sunlight on the rotting flesh, had said it was beautiful. Oh Christ, McAlmon said derisively. What posturing!

His derision upset me. What was the cause of it? What was he holding against Ernest? I reminded him that Baudelaire had written a good poem about a corpse. That cynical twisted grin came on his face. "Oh, sure," he jeered, "Hemingway probably read it too." While I argued with him he knew I was resisting his view of Ernest. I remembered that Ernest had once admired him enough to dedicate a book to him. It annoyed him and he got up and looked out the window and I joined him, asking if it was true the rue Vaugirard was the longest street in Paris. It was, he said. Coming back to Ernest, he told a scandalous story of something he claimed had happened between them on that trip back from Spain. And I remember thinking, Oh, Bob, you're all wrong even if you don't believe you're wrong. You wouldn't be talking this way if you weren't hurt. Is it that you think Ernest has forgotten that you helped him and hasn't tried to get you a publisher in New York?

Poor Bob, if he only could have restrained his malice when he thought he had been belittled; if he could only have known that he was wrong in thinking Ernest, in his success, had forgotten about him and wouldn't lift a hand to help him. Within a year, back in New York, I was to learn that Hemingway had persuaded Perkins at Scribner's to publish a book of McAlmon's. Yes, at lunch Perkins told me grimly there was something he wanted me to know about my friend McAlmon, whom I kept mentioning. As a favor to Hemingway, and only as a favor, mind you, they had planned to publish a novel of McAlmon's. McAlmon had come to New York for the inevitable lunch with Perkins. At this lunch McAlmon had told about the trip to Spain and his scandalous interpretation of an incident, not knowing that in his malice he was trying to destroy the man who was secretly helping him. Perkins said to me belligerently, "I tell you this because McAlmon is your friend. You too may have wondered if Hemingway forgot him. Well, he didn't." Then Perkins added sternly, "I don't care if you tell McAlmon why we're not publishing his book. I hope you do tell him." And I was silent and sad.

But there in McAlmon's hotel room I couldn't know what was going to happen. I remember he saw that he had upset me, and brushing aside the talk about Ernest, he became a quite charming man. Chuckling, he told me there were two "bright boys" from Montreal in the Quarter, and I should surely meet them, and he laughed. He gave me their names. He would leave word I was around. He suggested that I come and stay at this hotel and he would know where to look for me on his return to Paris. In the meantime he had to catch a train.

Leaving his hotel, I was gloomy, half convinced that writers couldn't go on being friends. Something would always happen that would make them shy away from each other. McAlmon had said Ernest now didn't want to have other writers as friends. In that case he wouldn't care whether or not he saw me. It could be that I was now just another writer, not an old friend.

That night Loretto and I, staying on the Right Bank, went to a movie where we were quickly reminded we were in Paris and not at home. The usher led us to a good seat. After we had been watching the movie for fifteen minutes the usher returned, asked to see our tickets, gave our seats to two other patrons who had tipped her, and led us back to the rear. So we had at least learned one thing in Paris: in a theatre you have to tip the usher. I told Loretto there was something else we might as well learn just as quickly: to feel at home in Paris all by ourselves. There was no reason why writers, admiring each other's works, should like each other personally, or even want to see each other. Let us, therefore, prepare ourselves to be on our own from now on. She, for her part, said she knew she was going to be happy in Paris whether or not we ever saw Fitzgerald or Hemingway, and even if McAlmon never came back. We would move to the Paris-New York Hotel tomorrow and look over our chosen neighborhood. And we did this. We moved to McAlmon's hotel. Just at twilight next day we were on our way up rue Vaugirard, and turning along Montparnasse by the station. For a few blocks Montparnasse was a dismal stretch of boulevard, but then we came to the Raspail corner and the cafés.

On one corner was the Dôme, which not long ago had been merely a zinc bar with a small terrace; now it was like the crowded bleachers at an old ball park, the chairs and the tables set in low rows extending as far as the next café, the Coupole. It had an even longer crowded terrace. Opposite the Dôme, on the other corner, was the Rotonde, where painters and a great many Scandinavians used to sit. Beside it, and by the intersecting side street, was a small new café.

An intersecting street separated it from the Sélect, which was open all night. We sat at the Coupole. The faces in rows there looked more international, whereas at the Dôme there seemed to be hundreds of recognizable Americans; men and women who, like us, had just got off the boat and were there for a night. Naturally we rejected all these too familiar faces. As it got darker the whole corner seemed to brighten and take on its own exotic life.

In those days they used to say if you sat there long enough you were bound to see someone you knew come strolling by. We watched and waited hopefully. We watched the taxis jammed at the corner making trouble for the gendarmes. It looked as if the taxi drivers were doing it deliberately, half taunting the gendarmes. It was to become such a familiar sight; there was, for example, to be the night when the drunken American poet, fighting with the gendarmes, got knocked cold. They were dragging him by the neck over the rough cobblestones; then the taxis, maneuvering, suddenly had the cops and their prey hemmed in, the taxi horns all hooting wildly, the traffic at the corner getting hopelessly snarled. The hemmed-in cops had to wait until the prostrate poet came to, so they could get him on his feet and let him have the dignity of walking away with them out of the taxi ring. In those days taxi drivers and artists seemed to have something in common.

But that first night, sitting there as strangers, wondering hopefully if Joyce, or Pound, or Fitzgerald or Ford, someone we would recognize, might pass by, we didn't feel lonely or out of place. The corner was like a great bowl of light, little figures moving into it and fading out, and beyond was all of Paris. Paris was around us and how could it be alien in our minds and hearts even if no Frenchman ever spoke to us?

What it offered to us was what it had offered to men from other countries for hundreds of years; it was a lighted place where the imagination was free. Men have to make room for such places in their thoughts even if they never visit them.

When we had had our fill of the faces and the snatches of conversation at the Coupole, we strolled along the boulevard as far as the Closerie des Lilas. How lovely the lighted tables spread out under the chestnut trees looked that April night; a little oasis of conviviality! Apollinaire's Café. We had a drink there under the trees and listened to a street singer and a fiddler till the weather suddenly turned cooler. Loretto wished she had worn a jacket. When she shivered we got up and walked away. Arm in arm we walked down the Boul' Mich, wondering why the big cafés were half deserted, cafés that in Oscar Wilde's time had been crowded, for this had been his territory. Every generation seemed to pick out its own territory in Paris, we agreed. Down at the Seine we stood for a long time together, watching the reflection of the colored lights on the river. Against the sky were the towers of Notre Dame. Oh, Catherine Medici, you Renaissance snob, why did you cut off those towers? Wandering along the quai I did the thing I used to do back home, whisper lines of Poe: "And thou wert all to me, love, a fountain and a shrine . . ." My father and mother read little prose, but I had grown up learning poetry by heart from them, and Poe was a great favorite in our house. And then as we stopped, watching the river, Loretto hummed, "I Can't Give You Anything But Love, Baby." We felt very confident and I said I would look up Hemingway tomorrow.

CHAPTER XI

The address we had was care of the Guaranty Trust Co. We didn't bother with it. In the afternoon we went to Shakespeare and Co., Sylvia Beach's famous bookshop on the rue de l'Odéon. Shakespeare and Co., which had published Joyce's *Ulysses*, was simply a good-sized, pleasant, uncommercial-looking bookstore. There was one rather large book-lined room, with another smaller one adjoining. At the desk sat a woman whom I knew, from pictures I had seen, to be Miss Beach. She was a fair, handsome woman in a severe suit, in her forties, I would have said; an Englishwoman; and in her manner there was something a bit severe and mannish. Yet she was an American. Having published *Ulysses*, she had become a famous woman. Writers in Paris, at least those who wrote in English, came often to her door. Her shop was a shrine for the Joyce lovers. Approaching the desk, I introduced myself and wondered if she could give me Hemingway's address. Without batting an eyelash, she told me she wasn't sure whether Hemingway was in town, nor if he were, whether she would be able to locate him before she heard from him. But if I would leave my own address she would make an effort to see that it was passed on.

Immediately I was unbelieving. The brush-off came a little too smoothly. Thanking her for the major effort I pretended to believe she would put forth, I rejoined Loretto and we busied ourselves seeing what books she had on her shelves. Suddenly Miss Beach left her desk and approached us. Had I seen the piece about my work in the *Harvard Hound and Horn?* she asked, handing it to me, then leaving us. "See," I whispered to my wife, "she knows who I am and she knows Hemingway's address and won't give it to me."

A section of the wall was taken over by a whole series of portraits of Joyce: as he was now with the heavy glasses, then as a student, a small boy, and even as a little baby. "I can understand her having a motherly feeling for Joyce," Loretto whispered, hiding her laughter, "since she's got him here with her in diapers. You should feel lucky. Supposing you had asked for Joyce?"

"To the devil with Miss Beach," I said. "Come on." Returning the *Hound and Horn* to Miss Beach's desk, we departed. No doubt she was right in protecting Hemingway from callers, just as she protected Joyce, but I was too young and arrogant to have respect for her consideration for her friends. In fact I was glad to hear from McAlmon a few weeks later that Miss Beach in her role of den mother sometimes made ridiculous mistakes. On one occasion, McAlmon told me, the great Irish writer, old George Moore, had come into her shop looking for Joyce. At the time Joyce had been browsing around in the back room. But Miss Beach, unyielding in her prim determination that Joyce should have a chance to screen the names of all prospective callers, had told Moore she would leave his name with Joyce. It didn't matter that Moore was leaving Paris next day. According to McAlmon, Joyce had been dismayed; it had seemed ridiculous to him that he had been left hidden a few yards away from a great Irishman he had always wanted to meet. My own name is not likely to be found in a memoir written by any of Miss Beach's coterie. On only one other occasion did I ever go back to her shop—to get a copy of Fitzgerald's *Great Gatsby*.

Disgruntled, we wandered away from the rue de l'Odéon. It would be necessary to write Ernest a note explaining that Mr. and Mrs. Callaghan were in residence at the Paris-New York Hotel on the rue Vaugirard, and hoped to hear from him. Well, why not? But we let two days pass without sending this note, half hoping Sylvia Beach might really have got in touch with him. The night of the second day we had been out till nearly dawn. Those two "bright little devils" Buffy and Graeme, McAlmon's friends, had come our way. Two slender boys in their early twenties, they were inseparable companions, very understanding of each other, soft spoken with a mocking opinion about everybody. They were writers. One of them had some money of his own, but not much. Within a few hours of meeting them we seemed to know ten or twelve other people at the café. And after being out all night we had slept till past noon, had eaten some croissants and coffee in our hotel room, and were sitting around when a knock came on the door. It was Hemingway. With him was his six-year-old boy, Bumbi. Ernest was wearing a dignified dark gray suit. He still had that old sweet charming smile. On his forehead was a new scar.

"Why, how are you?" I said, and we shook hands. I introduced my wife to him and his boy, and then as he entered the room slowly there was a moment of shyness when I felt like a stranger. I had on a dark brown velvet dressing gown which Loretto had given me as a present; it was expensive and looked like a crocodile skin. Stepping back, looking at me and shaking his head, Ernest said to Loretto, "I haven't seen such a dressing gown on a man since the last time I saw Georges Carpentier climb into the ring." That dressing gown saved us a lot of slow words. I asked him where he had picked up the scar on his forehead. Reluctantly, he told about an object falling through the skylight and hitting him on the head. And the strange part of it is—I remember this well— that having written so many stories myself, and having heard from him about them, and having read his stories, and heard too, the McAlmon view on him, which I simply didn't believe, as well as the stories of mutual friends in New York, I nevertheless seemed to know him better sitting there in this Paris hotel room then I ever had back home. We talked for a few minutes about Bumbi, a handsome boy. Ernest said he was on his way to Hadleys' place with Bumbi; Hadley was the wife he had had in Toronto; we could go with him, he said, then we could go to a café and have a drink.

On that slow walk up the rue Vaugirard with the sun coming out suddenly after the grayness of noontime, the little boy kept a step ahead so the three of us could walk abreast. Now, years later, Loretto asks, "Who was the fighter he started talking about? What was that fighter's name? Remember, he laughed about him and dismissed him, don't you remember?" But how did it come about that he started right in talking about fighters, going slowly up the street? Maybe he had asked me if I had seen any good fights lately. Or that he knew for sure I would have seen Larry Gains, this big Negro heavyweight in my own town. It was Gains we talked about. Ernest laughed derisively at Gains. He should know all about the Negro, he said. The fact was he, himself, had tried to manage Gains in Europe. No one though could do much with Gains. It made me feel abashed. This Negro fighter had seemed to me to be a very talented boy. I had seen him fight with Mike McTeague, the middleweight champion. A beautiful boxer who unfortunately couldn't take a punch. Already Ernest was making me feel I had never seen a really good fighter.

It is a long walk up to Montparnasse, and perhaps Ernest noticed that his boy was tiring. We got into a taxi, drove to Hadley's place, and while Ernest went in with the boy, we waited in the taxi. On his return he told the driver to take us to a café on the Boul' Mich. This café was right down at the corner by the quai. From the terrace you could see the river and the Isle de la Cité. As we sat down in the sunlight and he ordered the beers I looked at him cautiously. Loretto, knowing I was trying to feel sure of him, smiled at me. Naturally I was watching Ernest to see if I could notice any change in him, or discover any shift in his view of me. Would he say, "Well, years ago I knew you were going to be heard from"? And could I say to him, "That quality you had which I noticed five years ago, the quality that makes people want to make up stories about you, does it bother you now?" I was thinking now of his literary personality, the public view of him.

And there was another thing; it was the cause of the slight feeling of caution in both Ernest and me. What about all that Scribner promotion that linked my name with his? I knew how fiercely jealous he was of his own identity. Hadn't he tried to belittle Anderson to free himself from him, to make it plain he stood alone? Why shouldn't he now push me away from him? But Ernest was very smart about such things, and aside from the fact that we both knew he had read and praised my stories before he scored his own great success, I think he knew that I was the one who was being disastrously damaged by the Scribner promotion. So I didn't mention this promotion to him. I felt it was beneath me, and sitting there, he didn't mention it either. And from then on I was sure he would never raise the subject. And he never did.

Suddenly he told us he had become a Catholic. The girl he had married, Pauline, was Catholic. So there we were, three of the faithful. Perhaps I should have clasped his hand warmly. I only looked reflective. Then Loretto asked him how he had been able to get a divorce and marry within the Church. Wasn't it always difficult? It hadn't been difficult, he said, since his first wife, Hadley, had never been baptized. Oh yes, a bit of luck, we agreed. He felt very good about being a convert. But converts had always bored me. At that time in France there were many conversions among the intellectuals. Christian artists were finding new dignity and spiritual adventure in the neo-Thomism of Jacques Maritain. Most converts I had known had changed their faith but not their personalities or their temperaments, and since they usually gained enormous self-assurance from the new faith, I would find myself disliking them more than ever. Too often a dualism remained in them. A beautiful writer like Mauriac would have one of his women characters, while holding a lover in her arms, be aware of the blackheads on his nose, a reminder that even in an ecstatic moment the flesh ought to be seen in its worst light. He made me feel exuberantly pagan. My own problem was to relate a Christian enlighten-

ment to some timeless process of becoming. A disgust with
the flesh born of an alleged awareness of an approaching
doomsday bored me, as did the flash of light that gave a man
the arrogant assurance that he was the elect of God.

I remember how I looked at Ernest, ready to question him,
then I shrugged and smiled. There he sat, so full-blooded and
healthy. And he had been so unassertive in telling about his
conversion, no one could have imagined he would ever think
of himself as the elect of God. Perhaps he saw I was neither
impressed nor enthusiastic, for his manner changed. I mean
he suddenly was with me in my feeling about converts; he
seemed to be saying that he called himself a Catholic now
because he recognized that he really had been Catholic for
some time—by temperament. In New York later, I heard
someone at a party say mockingly, "Hemingway became a
Catholic because all the Spanish bullfighters were Catholic."
No. There was much more to it than that. At the café that
day, reflecting, watching his face as he talked, it struck me
that by some twist of temperament, in spite of his puritan
family, he was in fact intended to be a Mediterranean Catholic. And as it turned out, the older he got, the more often
death kept hovering over his stories; he kept death in his
work as a Medieval scholar might have kept a skull on his
desk, to remind him of his last end.

You only needed to look at his face, his eyes and his mouth,
to know that he delighted in all that was sensuous. He had
to savor all the sensations, know all the delights of the senses
—with death apparently in his imagination like a presiding
officer always asking him how he would take it when he came
to the end of his knowing. What was more natural now that
having established himself as an old hand in the faith, he
should quickly begin to share my indulgent air toward all

well-known converts. As old pros, whom did we pick on for our condescension? T. S. Eliot! We looked down our noses at his conversion. We shared our amusement over his choice of Anglo-Catholicism. Well, with the temperament he had it was probably the best Eliot could do. It was all very discreet and if it left him way out in left field, no harm was done.

Then Ernest told us about the new baby and asked if we wouldn't like to come to his house and see the boy. We told him we would. We were at ease. Within a few minutes I had felt all my old liking for him.

As we drank our beer I noticed that Ernest would empty his glass in a few gulps, then turn to me. "Have another beer?" I had kept up with him for three quick ones. I had always liked to drink beer slowly, and after the three I felt distended. Why the hell am I doing this? I asked myself. Though I kept my half-filled glass in my hand, and Ernest could see it was still half-filled, each time he ordered he would say, "Are you sure you won't have one?" The waiter leaves the saucer that comes with each drink on the table, so he can count them up for you when you are leaving and show you what you owe him. Soon Ernest had a pile of seven saucers to my three.

When he had left us, I turned to Loretto. "Well, how do you like him?"

"Very much. You can't help liking him. Tell me, has he changed at all?"

"No, he hasn't changed at all—except for one thing."

"What's that?"

"Didn't you notice about the beer and how he made it plain I couldn't keep up with him? Now he just has to be the champ."

CHAPTER XII

He lived at 6 rue Ferou, which was within a quarter of a mile of the St. Sulpice Cathedral—this fact comes into the story later. He had a living room off a narrow room with a long oaken table, and, I suppose, a kitchen and some bedrooms. On the wall was a Joan Miró painting of a fish. The great Miró was his friend, he said. With some pride he showed us a small Goya he had been able to smuggle out of Spain.

When he went back to speak to his wife, we looked around the living room. The furniture might have been all of a period. By the window was an antique table, but what took our eye was a Spanish chair with the largest grandest curving back I had ever seen. Returning, and still by himself, Ernest led us into a little nursery. I remember his half-proud, half-shy and boyishly awkward shrug as he said, "Well, if you're interested in babies, there he is . . ." The dark-haired child was indeed plump and beautiful. While Ernest and I watched, my wife played with the child, and such an occasion is a time for silence on the part of watching men.

Then Pauline came into the living room, followed by a maid bringing tea and sandwiches on a tray which she put on the table by the window, and, of course, as soon as I turned to her, I remembered how Ernest had praised his first wife, Hadley the musician. This was the one who had taken Hadley's place. Pauline, a small woman with dark brown hair and a good complexion, wasn't a beauty, but she was pleasant-faced and steady-eyed. She had firmness or quiet determination in her expression. As soon as she shook hands I knew she had no intention of going overboard for us. Polite, courteous, yes. But after all, she seemed to say in her manner, just what did we expect? What could I mean to Ernest, or want of him, unless, well . . .

But Loretto and Pauline could smile warmly at each other as they delighted in the baby. That day Loretto was wearing a kind of high white straw Cleopatra hat and a silk suit, a short coral skirt, a coat with a black and white zigzag pattern, and lined with coral; a suit she had made herself. The suit took Pauline's eye. Having been a fashion writer for *Vogue,* she went straight to the point. Loretto had got the suit in Paris, of course? No? She had made it herself? Oh? Well, at least she had got the hat here. It was indeed a Paris hat, Loretto admitted, but she had got it back home. A little surprised, Pauline said it was lovely. The great trick in Paris, she said, was to pick up these hats very cheaply from little unknown milliners who had great style. As a matter of fact, she knew of a comparatively unknown milliner who was wonderful. Did Loretto want her address? It may have been that

Loretto sounded merely gratefully appreciative rather than warmly eager, for Pauline, after taking the trouble to get a pencil and a piece of paper, and have Loretto stand at the window so she could give her directions, said abruptly, "Are you sure you really want to use this milliner? I won't bother giving you the name unless you really intend to go there." It was a blunt and startling challenge. The look coming into Loretto's brown eyes was familiar to me. But she affirmed quickly and solemnly she had every intention of hurrying directly to the milliner. Pauline wrote down the name.

Whether Ernest had been listening as closely as I had to the little dialogue between the two wives, I don't know. But he turned to me as he sat down, and apparently at random, just to make conversation, asked if I had ever done any boxing. Yes, I had done quite a bit of boxing, I said truthfully. "Just a minute," he said quietly and he left the room. While he was gone I drank a cup of tea. Then Ernest reappeared with a set of boxing gloves. "Come one, let's see," he said, holding out a pair of gloves to me.

"Oh, come on," I said, refusing the gloves. Then suddenly I remembered the comment he had made to the mutual friend about my fight story in Scribner's; nobody was any better than Morley when he stuck to the things he knew something about. I seemed to know then intuitively that quite aside from his interest in my career, or any changes that might have taken place in my personality since he had seen me, he had this one little curiosity about me. It is these little questions about each other that are at the root of most men's relationships. Suppose I had been faking an interest in fighters? Would it mean the loss of his respect for me? But this little thing, this little question, must have been in the back of his mind when he came to our hotel room. The crack

about the Georges Carpentier dressing gown! And wasn't
it why he had started talking about that Negro fighter, Larry
Gains, getting my opinion of him as we walked up the street?
And maybe, even when we were talking about his own conversion, he had been looking at me, his curiosity gnawing
away at him. Not my work, or my life, just this one detail!
What a strange man, I thought, looking at him. Calm, untroubled, just a little amused, he waited, holding out the
gloves. Was he making a point about writing? Was it why
we hadn't talked so far about his writing or mine? "Come on,
put them on," he insisted.

"Here in this room?"

"Just put them on. I want to see," he said.

Trying to laugh in my embarrassment, I looked around the
room. The tea tray was on the table by the window. But the
Spanish chair with the great curving back was close to me.
Loretto, alarmed, mystified, also tried to laugh. "You can't
box here," she said. Pauline, though, had made no protest, in
fact she seemed to be interested. Then I felt annoyed; he had
asked me if I had ever boxed; why wouldn't he take my
word for it? Feeling like a fool, I got up, wondering what
would happen if we lurched against the Spanish chair and
shattered it. I pulled on the gloves. Raising my hands as he
raised his, we squared off.

Unless I had to, I didn't want to move around and fall in
Loretto's lap. How could I know what would happen? He
lunged at me with a left and I ducked, and then he swung
a right at me which I blocked. Rooted in our positions, both
showing the same respect for the Spanish chair, we made
some more passes at each other. And it was ridiculous. But
suddenly he appeared to be satisfied. A real glow of pleasure
came on his face, and he began to pull off his gloves. "I only

wanted to see if you had done any boxing," he said apologetically. "I can see you have." He ignored the fact that he hadn't taken my word for it. Yet his pleasure was so genuine I was immediately mollified. The doubt he had had about me seemed to have vanished.

When we were seated and laughing, he suggested eagerly that we go boxing. Nobody around the Quarter could really box, he said. He had been missing his boxing. Not far away was the American Club. It had no ring, but there was lots of space. Would I call for him tomorrow late in the afternoon? Everything then was fine. In a little while we left.

But outside Loretto took a slightly different tone. "Isn't that Pauline a blunt one?" she said loftily. "Just imagine. Her time is so valuable she can't write down the address of a milliner unless I take an affidavit I'll use it. What's the matter with her?"

"Well, she liked your own hat anyway."

"Oh, just because she could see it was a Paris hat," Loretto said airily. "You know, a lot of those fashion writers haven't much style themselves. Well, I had a feeling about Pauline. Perhaps I'm wrong, but I felt something. I felt Pauline is prepared to resist us. Not put herself out in any way. She's read all that silly Scribner stuff about you and Hemingway. Oh sure, Ernest may have told her all about you, but she's not fooled. Nobody's edging in on Ernest while she's around. It's a very big thing for her to be Ernest's wife, you know."

"Come on now. For her Ernest became a Catholic."

"You said he should be a Catholic anyway."

"I said he could see himself as a Catholic. I wonder what Pauline would have said if we had lurched around and broken her furniture?"

CHAPTER XIII

Next day I called for Ernest. He was carrying a bag containing the boxing gloves and his gym shoes, and I had in my hand a pair of those French rope-soled espadrilles as we loafed along the street. And I remember we talked about the Irish novelist, Liam O'Flaherty, whose book *The Informer* I had liked very much, and who had written a novel called *Mr. Gilhooley*. Ernest agreed that *The Informer* was a fine book, but in *Mr. Gilhooley*, O'Flaherty had made a mistake; he had started thinking too much. A writer always got into trouble when he started thinking on the page. He permitted the reader to see that the character was being forced to do the author's thinking. I began to be charmed. Walking so slowly, engaged completely in each other's opinion, I could see that Ernest had the same firm tone, the same utter conviction he had five years ago. It was as if no time had passed; nothing

had happened to either one of us. I argued with him, Wasn't
he rejecting a whole aspect of life? Surely he would agree
that a metaphysical problem could be part of a man's life.
Maybe so, but he shook his head grudgingly; he distrusted
methaphysics, all abstract thought. The job of the writer was
to deal in what was concrete, what a character could feel,
and taste and touch, and his thinking should go along with
this immediacy of things. No, that last phrase is wrong; he
couldn't have talked about "the immediacy of things." Just
the same, in those days he didn't use the strange dumb-
Indian talk he palmed off years later on interviewers. He expressed himself rather slowly but very accurately. A
character, a pure intellectual, he went on, doing his thinking
on the page, well, it was pretty hard for the author to keep
out of it. The story should be the thing. Shaking his head,
he clammed up, wouldn't go on talking about metaphysics;
he distrusted the whole speculative process. But I had taken
law. I had studied philosophy a little and I liked arguing
about ideas. If we were two Christian gentlemen and artists
out for a stroll in Paris we ought to have been able to talk,
say, about Maritain's *Art and Scholasticism*. But Ernest had
an artist's, not a philosopher's, interest in art. To this day
someone will say, "Hemingway didn't seem to have much of
an education." By this, I suppose, the academic critic means
Ernest hadn't taken his own formal academic drill. But as the
philosophers themselves are aware, the artist kind of knowing, call it intuition if you will, could yield a different kind
of knowledge beyond rational speculation. Anyway, Ernest
read everything.

We had come to the American Club, where Ernest seemed
to be at home. We went downstairs and into a back room
that had a cement floor. In one corner of the room were some

mats and the parallel bars. This was the room the members evidently used for a little gym exercise. In an adjoining room was a billiard table. Some fellows were playing. They paid no attention to us. Ernest and I stripped down to our shorts and shirts. I tied on my espadrilles, he put on his gym shoes. We began to box.

In the back of my mind were all the stories I had heard of Hemingway's skill and savagery. That one story Max Perkins had told me about Hemingway jumping into the ring and knocking out the middleweight champion of France with a single punch made me feel apprehensive. And the way he had looked down his nose at Larry Gains! Ernest was big and heavy, over six feet, and I was only five foot eight and fat. Whatever skill I had in boxing had to do with avoiding getting hit. Admittedly I had a most unorthodox style, carrying my gloves far too low, counting on being fast with my hands. Moving around, crouching, bobbing and weaving, I waited for a chance to counterpunch. I was a little afraid of Ernest. All the lore and legend of the pros seemed to be in his stance; and in the way he held his hands, his chin down a little to his shoulder, he made an impressive picture. Watching him warily, I could only think, Try and make him miss, then slip away from him. All I did for the first three-minute round was slip away. Resting a minute, we chatted affably, then went on with it.

Suddenly he rushed me, loomed up over me, big and powerful, got me in a corner where I crouched lower and lower, all covered up like a turtle in its shell. Then he stopped, smiling. "Look, Morley," he said patiently, "never crouch that low. It's impossible to punch from that angle," and there he was, giving me kindly instructions. As I listened I was dreadfully humiliated.

I'm not trying to box with him, I thought with disgust at myself. I'm trying to defend myself against all the wild legends I've heard—against the man who tried to make something out of big Larry Gains. Yet all winter long I had been boxing with my friend Joe Mahon, who, just as big as Ernest, had been the international intercollegiate heavyweight champion. Concealing the disgust I felt for myself, I assured Ernest he wouldn't find me doubled up, almost on my knees, in the corner again.

I soon found out I could hit him easily. Seeing that I was carrying my left far too low, he would half jab with his left then try the right, but his timing was way off. I would draw him closer by feinting a step backward, inviting him to move in with his long left, then step in and beat him to the punch with my own left. His right, coming at me correctly, was too slow. I was catching him on the mouth or jaw. As the round progressed I became at ease and sure of myself. I could see that, while he may have thought about boxing, dreamed about it, consorted with old fighters and hung around gyms, I had done more actual boxing with men who could box a little and weren't just taking exercise or fooling around. Since I could see this for myself, it didn't matter to me that he would never believe it.

How did he take it, my left flicking all the time at his mouth and nose? One of the legends I had heard was that he grew savage when hurt and had to kill. It was plainly nonsense and dreadfully unfair to him. That day he took a punch on the nose like any good college boxer; he took it with grace and an appreciation of the aptitude of the man who had landed it. It may have been that he felt he had helped me, got me going with the instructions about not crouching too low. He certainly had; he had hurt my pride. He couldn't have known my thoughts.

When we had called it a day and were taking a shower, he was extraordinarily happy and full of good spirits. We went out for a drink.

The small café had only three tables on the sidewalk. We talked for awhile about sports. For some reason I had assumed that he had been good at football and baseball, so I talked about ballplayers and my years as a pitcher, and asked what position he had played. But he said he had only played ball a little, and had never been really good at team sports. He liked skiing and boxing and fishing and shooting, the solitary sports. The things a man could do alone. Then I asked him if Fitzgerald was in town. Not that he knew of, he said. As far as he knew the Fitzgeralds would not be in Paris for a few weeks. He volunteered no further information about Scott, so I dropped the subject.

In a happy mood, I tried in my best comic style to talk about our mutual friends on the *Star*. Listening, he barely smiled. So I swung into some of my most amusing stories about Harry Hindmarsh. Ernest had said that he would one day write a book about Hindmarsh and call it *The Son in Law*. By his silence he made it clear he no longer had to hate Hindmarsh. He made me feel, too, that I was talking about people and things that belonged to a time long ago. Untouched, impassive, so darkly hidden as he listened, he became like a stranger. This gift of sudden complete withdrawal was new. It worried me. Coming out of it suddenly, he told me he liked Loretto very much; she was a fine girl, and then with the old frankness I had always liked in him, he added, "She has a kind of savage candor, hasn't she?" Instantly I wondered what Pauline had said to him about that

milliner, or had he too noticed that Pauline's bluntness had taken Loretto aback? Or could it have been that he had been surprised when Loretto asked him how he had managed to get married in the Church? But since we were on delicate ground I made no comment other than I had thought he would like Loretto. And of course I said we liked Pauline too.

Reaching down to the bag in which he carried the boxing gloves, he asked me if I would like to glance at the proofs of *A Farewell to Arms*. Right now, he said, he was taking the proofs to James Joyce. Ordering another drink, he waited, asking no questions while I read the first two chapters. I noticed the change in style since *The Sun Also Rises*. But the magic was in the way the words came cleanly together; the landscape was done with his painter's eye, not Cézanne's eye, his own, and I recalled that back in Toronto he had told me that he wished sometimes he had been a painter. Yet here was a little trait I noticed, a continuation of a trend that I, maybe wrongly, had marked in *The Sun Also Rises*. I had felt in my bones that Hemingway himself was going to be identified with his hero, Jake Barnes. Now the identification would be pinned on Lieutenant Henry. Readers would be convinced that everything happening to the lieutenant had happened to Hemingway, and his literary personality would grow apace. Was this what he wanted? Would there ever be a showdown between himself as he was and this growing literary personality? It bothered me.

In the beginning I had been sure Hemingway would be a broad objective writer like Tolstoy. Was he to become an intensely personal writer, each book an enlargment of his personality in the romantic tradition? Well, a good writer goes his own way. But sitting there with him at the little café, all in the shadow now for the sunlight had gone, I did wonder if he was to make all his work seem like a personal adventure. Then I tried to express my admiration of the descriptive prose; it was to be a bigger book than *The Sun Also Rises*, I said, and I remember that as he picked up the proofs he laughed. "*The Sun Also Rises* was the kind of book you write in six weeks," he said. Just the same, I said, rarely had a book been so warmly received by reviewers, and, marvelous to relate, rarely had they been so right. Growing more serious, talking with that intensity of conviction that had always made me feel he had a vast store of secret wisdom about writing, he said, "Always remember this. If you have a success, you have it for the wrong reasons. If you become popular it is always because of the worst aspects of your work. They always praise you for the worst aspects. It never fails."

It was comforting; it was encouraging; it was like knowing that he would never be taken in by spurious adulation, or let the mob make him anything but the fine artist he was. Closing my eyes now, I can see us sitting at that café, hearing him talk about becoming popular because of the weakest aspects of one's work. Now, remembering, it becomes deeply moving.

We had got up and were walking slowly along the street. At the corner he said, "I'll leave you here. I'm late. I told Joyce I'd bring these proofs to him." And then he must have seen an envious look in my eyes. Suddenly he was boyishly apologetic. "I know you'd like to meet Joyce. I'd take you with me and have you meet him, Morley, but he's so shy with strangers. It's no good when you walk in on him. He won't talk about writers and writing. This way it wouldn't be any good. You understand, don't you?"

"Of course I do," I said. "I wouldn't dream of going with you. You want to talk to him about your work," and I laughed. We made a date for boxing the next week. He went one way and I another up to the Sélect to meet Loretto. When I looked back he was going along slowly, carrying his bag, a big fellow, feeling good.

If I couldn't meet Joyce with him it wasn't likely I would ever meet him, I thought. And then suddenly I felt my own peaceful satisfaction. After five years, there I was on a Paris street; in spite of the stories, the malice, my own doubts, I was watching the retreating figure of the man who had been so quick and generous in his appreciation of my work, and we had had an immensely enjoyable afternoon together.

CHAPTER XIV

Our room in the Paris-New York Hotel overlooked a side street. It was always late in the morning when we got up, but we were never too late to see a little funeral procession, a quaint hearse and an equally quaint-hatted driver and a handful of black-clad mourners, following the hearse. Men passing on the street would always take off their hats. Loretto might be young and blooming, and I might be feeling pretty good myself, but death indeed was always there, just around the corner. I have said that Ernest, always keeping the thought of death in his work, reminded me of a Medieval scholar who kept the skull on his desk to remind him of his last end. With my girl close to me I preferred to consider the lilies of the field. I was a great caster of bread on the waters. Does the dolphin or the rose flourish with an eye on eternity? Death for me was a painful, gloomy, inevitable experience.

As for the Greek who said, "Better never to have been born," I thought he was kidding. Our job, I used to say to Loretto, was to be concerned with living and it seemed to me it would be most agreeable to God if we tried to realize all our possibilities here on earth, and hope we would always be so interested, so willing to lose ourselves in the fullness of living, and so hopeful that we would never ask why we were on this earth. Therefore, it was pointless to have those little funeral processions with our breakfast. We decided to move, and quickly.

Our new friends, the two boys, Buffy and Graeme, helped us to find an apartment. They sat with us at the café, reading the advertisements in the newspaper. We found an apartment over a grocery store on the rue de la Santé, near the prison. Our landlady, a handsome, carrot-topped, buxom Russian in her rapidly fading forties, had only a few words of English and not much more French. Now that we were established we fell into a routine. We would get up around noon, walk slowly over to the Coupole, have a little lunch on the terrace, then go across the river to the American Express to inquire for mail. Sometimes we loafed around the Right Bank for two hours, having a drink at some café by the Opéra, or the Madeleine, then making some purchase in the Galerie Lafayette, then on to the Champs Elysées where the sunlight was on the trees. In the daytime we never went to Montmartre, only at night when we went to Zelli's or dropped into Bricktop's. But Paris was always in our minds as a very satisfying and beautiful picture, the soft river valley, the gentle slopes, the two hills, and on the Right Bank sunlight on the white dome of Sacré Coeur.

Back at the apartment I would work for a couple of hours, then at six we could be seen coming down the street by the long prison wall, turning and passing the Observatoire, then the Lilas, and on to the Coupole for an *apéritif* and some conversation. My friendship with Hemingway seemed to give us an anchor beyond our own neighborhood. At least once a week I would see him for boxing. Afterwards the two of us would walk up to the Sélect to meet Loretto and have a drink. How quick and interested would be his rebuke if we found her having a glass of Pernod. "Loretto, you shouldn't be drinking that stuff. Don't drink it," he would complain. "I'm only taking the one drink," she would protest.

At that time he would never come wandering around the cafés by himself; he had given it up. And besides, Pauline had conveyed to us her belief that café sitting was a little beneath her. For our part we were not concerned with the impression we might be making, nor with the fact that French ladies of quality did not sit at the cafés. Often I would mention Fitzgerald to Ernest. Had he any word of Scott being in town? It was still in my mind that Perkins had said Scott and Ernest were the greatest of friends. Ernest would say he had had no word of Scott. I never told him how much I looked forward to meeting Scott, nor did I tell him of the picture I had had of the three of us being together and enjoying each other's company. That day would soon come, I was sure.

By ten in the evening Loretto and I, established at our table at the Sélect, might remain there with friends for hours, or we might go to a party. There was always a party, someone leaving or someone returning. Many a night we spent with young unknown painters who would ask us to their studios to see their work. Now that I look back on it, those good times, good conversations with young painters, must have come about because neither Loretto nor I had the regular critical patter. We could only talk to them about what we saw and felt ourselves in a canvas. They seemed to love it; one canvas after another, the young painter watching us and listening with a little gleam in his eye.

In our neighborhood many of the painters and writers were desperately poor. Yet at that time, in the world of that time, there was the certainty that loose money was close at hand, even if it was in someone else's pocket. In New York the stock market always seemed to be going up. If you weren't in on it, it was because you preferred the quest for new experience. That particular quest, the drive of the idler, the bum, the artist—the quest for some new experience! The morality of the experience was measured by its novelty; the charm, the virtue of novelty. Yet the Quarter was an aristocracy. A rich man had no distinction and no real power. I remember the night in a bar with McAlmon and a rich young American who was living a life of splendid idleness in the Quarter; when it came time to pay the bill after hours of drinking, McAlmon, indicating the young rich man, said ruthlessly, "No, let him pay. He's along with us, isn't he?" It was even more humiliating when the young businessman quickly and quietly paid for all the drinks.

Why had this young Chicago businessman settled in Paris? He happened to be "a lover of the arts." Some years earlier Sherwood Anderson in *Dark Laughter* had told how a "wonderful and terrible thing had happened in Paris." It was the wide-eyed Midwestern view of the city for those who had the money and the time for a holiday fling. For other Americans there had been the grand discovery of European culture, another way of living, a promise of some enlargement of inner freedom. A whisper had gone the rounds that Greenwich Village was washed up: Paris was the new frontier. In the early twenties living had been inexpensive, and if you wanted to be a publisher and have a little magazine the printing costs were cheap. Above all, Paris was the good address. It was the one grand display window for international talent, and if you were at all interested in the way the intellectual cloth of the time was being cut you had to be there, even if you couldn't do more than press your nose against the window.

Looking back on it, what American writer of the twenties or thirties, or the fifties, from Gertrude Stein to Faulkner to Henry Miller or Tennessee Williams didn't feel compelled to drop into the great style center to look around. It is not quite the same today. New York has challenged the Paris influence, and Rome has come into the picture and so has London. But some of the magic still remains in the word from Paris. If you want to know what it was like in the late twenties you only have to recall what has gone on in the forties and fifties. How these French writers get blown up so the international public is persuaded to listen and believe something new is being said is probably a carefully guarded French national trade secret. Through the late forties and fifties; now is the time for the writer to be engaged with society; then later; now is the time for disengagement. And Existentialism! Today in the North American universities thousands of students are worrying and wondering if there is anything new in Existentialism, or perhaps deciding that they too ought to look at the world with Sartre's "disgust and anguish."

The word from Paris. It's not the voice of the turtle today but it was in the twenties. It offered the climate, the ambience, the importance of the recognition of the new for the artist. In those days a writer coming to Paris could believe he would find contemporaries and it didn't seem to matter to him that the French themselves paid no attention to him. In no time you learned that the oddly parochial French took it for granted you were absorbed in their culture. If not, what were you doing there in their style center? Stealing a style or two? Why not? It was the international custom. The burglars of French literature and painting.

We are born, we live a while, and we die, and along the way the artist keeps looking at the appearance of things, call it concrete reality, the stuff of experience, or simply "what is out there." Now I think that for intellectuals, writers and artists, the Paris of those days had become like a giant crystal; like a crystal with many facets, and the French had a genius for turning and ever turning the crystal so the light would fall on a new facet, and then from the cafés would come the announcement, "This is the way it is being looked at now." Naturally the writer or painter in far-off cities is charmed and interested. And yet, when you think about it, the question arises, "Were any of those French writers of the time, aside from the intellectual gowns they were wearing, as good as the strangers in town? Cocteau, Breton, Aragon and Co.? In a sense they were in the millinery business. And the great Gide? He was a moralist, he sounded the moral tone, or rather the tone of no morality at all beyond the aesthetic approach to life. His great strength was in his stylish comment on life, not in the creation of it. But Joyce and Hemingway, the foreigners, were to have a world influence. And just as in the nineteenth century the world capital for the novelist turns out to have been Moscow, well, where was it in twenty-nine?

The capital did seem to be in Paris, sitting at the café with the young businessman. The marks of the quick and wonderful French intelligence seemed to be all around one in this city with its open beauty, its elegance, and that splendid indifference of the French citizen at the next table to your private life. And above all, in every corner of this lovely Babylonian capital was stuck the national symbol, the shrewd-eyed watchful madame at the cash register. I could see her there in black near the café door, reminding me of the eternal verities.

By ten in the evening the whole corner would take on the fullness of its own life with the terraces crowded and the well-known drunken poets or painters, celebrated for their stupor rather than their art, wandering across the road from café to café, making the taxis dodge them. A tourist bus would pass, the tourists gawking, and Flossie Martin, the ex-Follies girl, plump, but still golden-haired and pink-and-white complexioned, who refused to go home to the States, would stand up and yell out an obscenity at the staring tourists in their bus. Or a visiting movie star, like Adolph Menjou, would be sitting at the Coupole with his new wife. While people lined up and moved slowly by his table where he sat, incredibly impassive, we, watching him from across the road, would snicker patronizingly. In the neighborhood was an American Jewish writer named Ludwig Lewisohn, who had written a successful book *Upstream* and had gone on to do novels. He looked like an important elderly professor. His friends, so I heard, had persuaded him to "show himself to the people," so now he would come slowly along the street. The others? Hundreds of others! Lawrence Vail, so blond and so sunburned; Kay Boyle. Michael Arlen, then rich and famous, having written *The Green Hat*, would be there with his beautiful wife, the Grecian countess. I liked Arlen. A shrewd, cynical, dapper dark man, he knew exactly what he was doing. For him, D. H. Lawrence was the only writer in the world and not to be compared with other writers. "The man is willing to live in a mud hut so he can write," he would say. Disdainful of this opinion, I argued with him. "You need a haircut," he said, looking at me quizzically. "You'd better get it cut or you'll think it's a halo."

We had got used to the night street cries, too. Cheerful little old women, selling newspapers, would cry out, *"Ami du Peuple."* A male newspaper vendor hurrying by would be muttering in a deep hoarse voice, *"Intransigeant, Paris Soir, Paris Soir."* Another vendor in a high falsetto voice, *"Chocolat, fruits glacés, cacahouettes, messieurs, dames."* Walking home at two in the morning we would pass that crowded little dance hall, The Jockey, with the jazz blowing from the open door. One night three little girls came skipping out, giggling and pushing each other. They were trying to sing the American popular song, "Constantinople." On the street, just ahead of us, they would shout out, "Constantinople" and as the song required, try to spell it out—"C-O-N-S-T-" and get no further. Shoving each other, they screamed with laughter.

On the way home we might pass Ford Madox Ford, the plump and portly president of a whole group of writers, who would be taking the night air all by himself, his hands linked behind his back. Old Ford, as Hemingway called him. Why did I always feel a little ashamed of my lack of sympathy for him; the friend of Henry James, the collaborator of Joseph Conrad? I had called him "Ford of many models." I hadn't felt drawn to him that time I had met him in New York; maybe it was his portly and heavy-mustached aloofness, his whispering voice. Yet I knew no man loved good contemporary writing more than he did. And one night at a dinner I heard him make a remark I have never forgotten: "No writer can go on living in a vacuum." It took me some years to discover how true this was; not just of writers, but of all men who would stay alone in their hearts. There must be someone somewhere you count on for approval, someone whose praise would be dear to you. When finally there is no one you might as well hand in your ticket.

My resistance to Ford, I think, came from seeing that he was a confessed literary man. On the theme of Ford and "the literary life," I remember one night when Loretto and I went to Ford's place for an evening with Allen Tate, his wife, Caroline Gordon, and the poet Leonie Adams. We were there, I imagined, for some talk and drinking. But to my astonishment Ford brought out a cake with white icing. "Since we're all literary people," he whispered, "we'll compete for this cake with sonnets. It goes to the one who writes the best sonnet." Allen Tate and Leonie Adams, accomplished poets, could dash off an acceptable sonnet at the drop of a hat. But as I began my sonnet my eyes were not on the paper but on Ford, who was scribbling away busily. My ball-playing days were only five years away. What would those tough ballplayers think, seeing me here in a sonnet competition for a stale cake? What was there to do but clown? "With Ford beside me groping in the dark, Oh, would that I were strolling in the park," I wrote with some malice. The sonnets having been finished, Ford read them aloud solemnly, including my ridiculous effort, which brought no smile to his face. We agreed that Leonie Adams had performed most elegantly.

But Ford was no fool. Those pale eyes of his were always on someone. And later, when we were out eating in a restaurant, he took a dig at me. "I'm sure Mr. Callaghan would have appreciated it more if we had had a story contest." I snorted scornfully. We were all snobs, of course. But if he had proposed a story contest I would have fled. When I think of this man now, I hear voices. On the street, the voice of

the pretty young woman from New York who had sat beside
Ford at dinner, and she was half crying, "What's the matter
with being an interior decorator? Why should Ford be insulting to me about it?" And my own voice saying to Hemingway, "Being gassed in the war gave Ford a great
advantage. We have to lean forward attentively when he
whispers." And Hemingway's derisive voice, "Gassed in the
war? Don't let him kid you. He was never gassed in the
war." Yet Ford had his coterie. Someone was always saying
he was one of the great modern masters of English prose. A
scholarship student named Bandy said belligerently, "Will
you argue this matter of Ford's prose with a man I'll name?"

"Sure," I said. "Who's your man?"

"Allen Tate," he said. "I'll show up with Tate at the Coupole tomorrow afternoon. Be there."

I remember saying to my wife, "I don't know how I can
train for this bout. This Tate is very scholarly and intelligent
and no doubt very fast on his feet, and I don't know whether
I should keep moving around him or get in close and hang
on."

At the appointed hour at the café there was Tate, sitting
with Bandy. In New York I had met the Southern poet with
the great domed head and the tapering chin. When we had
had a drink, we gingerly got to the question: was Ford a
great prose writer? Rather mildly, and with a complete lack
of passion, Tate suggested that *The Good Soldier* was a
pretty good book. Now this book has for an opening sen-
tence, "This is the saddest story I ever heard." Was it the
saddest story Tate had ever heard? I wondered aloud. No, it
wasn't, he said. Could we agree then on a writer who had a
great prose style? Yes, Swift. We agreed on Swift. As I recall
it, Ford was somehow quickly forgotten, and the promoter of
the bout, Bandy, remained silent and crestfallen as if the

light had gone out suddenly on his main event.

But at parties where Ford was, there was usually a crowd; people always meeting and parting. At one big party an Australian woman was either saying good-bye to Ford or meeting him once more, but I remember only that she was crying. At this party that important, middle-aged and humorless writer named Ludwig Lewisohn came over to me. It was time we knew each other, he said. We should have a talk. A great idea, I agreed. I would be sitting at the Coupole at two the following afternoon. And indeed, I was there.

Before Lewisohn's arrival, the young American named Whidney, from Chicago, who lived with his wife in an opulent apartment a few blocks away from the café, came and sat down beside me. "Do you mind if I sit in on this?" he asked. "I heard you and Lewisohn talking last night. I've read his book *Upstream*. I'd like to listen in on your conversation, if you don't mind. I promise I'll just sit here and listen."

Then Lewisohn came slowly along the street, looking very dignified, very professorial, his hat severely straight on his head. When I waved to him, he came and sat down with us. The conversation went like this: "Well, now, how is your book doing, Mr. Callaghan?"

"All right, I think," I said.

"How long has it been out?"

"Just a few months."

"Don't they let you know how it's doing?"

"It's had a good reception. But it's a book of stories, you know. With some luck, I think it'll reach five thousand."

"Five thousand," he said, looking distressed. "With all the publicity you've had? Five thousand?"

"It's a book of stories. How's your novel doing?"

"Why, it's already done thirty thousand."

"Splendid," I said, feeling like a nobody.

"But I expect to do much better than thirty thousand," he said importantly. We began an earnest discussion about sales promotion, and kept it up till my friend Whidney suddenly cut in. "Excuse me. Will you excuse me?" he asked firmly. "I have something to say."

"Go ahead."

"I was present when you two met last night. Well, I was a businessman, myself. I wanted to be here when you great artists talked. I thought it would be intellectually stimulating. You know what you sound like? A couple of businessmen."

Giving Whidney one long appraising glance, Mr. Lewisohn then finished his drink, left Whidney hanging there, reached out, patted me on the arm and said he had an appointment. As he walked away briskly, I, who had been told that he had always been of two minds about sitting at cafés, knew we wouldn't see him on the terrace again.

The terrace. A whole life went on there, a life in the open, the talented and the useless, living in each other's pockets, living on each other's dreams, and living in comical backbiting rather than love. Men and women from all over Europe, mingled with the Americans, most of them splendidly unknown. A position of dignity and importance was held by "the greatest unknown writer." And publishers and agents passing through would try to get word of the mysterious champion, whoever he was. But Joyce never came to the cafés. I used to wonder if Fitzgerald, on his return, would avoid the corner, too. As for Hemingway, as I said, all that summer he only came to the corner to have a drink with Loretto and me after boxing.

CHAPTER XV

Ernest and his boxing! After the events I'm relating had occurred, Ernest back in the States could say to Josephine
Herbst, "But my writing is nothing. My boxing is everything." When Miss Herbst told this to me I laughed, but was
full of wonder. That a great artist like Ernest could have
such a view of himself seemed incredible. Yet in the strange
dark depths of his being he had to pretend to believe it. For
the sake of the peace of their own souls most men live by
pretending to believe in something they secretly know isn't
true. It seems to be a dreadful necessity. It keeps life going
on. We agree especially to pretend to believe in things that
can never be known. Each civilization seems to have derived
some creative energy from an agreement upon the necessity
of a general pretending. Why it was necessary for Ernest to
pretend to believe that his boxing was the root of his whole
life, I don't know. It is true some men are much better at
pretending than others. It's a built-in gift. The game for

them takes on a reality that shapes their whole lives.

I had discovered that Ernest's attitude to his boxing was related to the source of his power as an imaginative writer. His imaginative work had such a literal touch that a whole generation came to believe he was only telling what he, himself, had seen happen, or what had actually happened to him. His readers made him his own hero. As he grew older it must have had tragic disadvantages for him. Now it seems to me that he shared with Sherwood Anderson, at least in this matter of his boxing, a matter of vital importance to his whole view of himself, a strange trick of the imagination—the built-in gift.

The night my wife and I went to dine with Anderson in the Washington Mews, where he was staying, we all sat around a long table after dinner, drinking and talking till two in the morning. We talked about many things. Hemingway's name came into the conversation. Next day I was meeting Max Perkins. As soon as he saw me he said, "I hear you had an interesting evening with Sherwood last night. I hear you made a splendid defense of Hemingway's Catholicism." Defend it! A look of indignant consternation must have come on my face. "Why, I never mentioned it. Why—" Taking my arm, Perkins said urgently, "Now just a minute. Before you go any further, please let me explain something to you. Don't let this spoil Sherwood for you. It's happened with others. You must understand Sherwood wasn't really lying . . ." Surely I would understand that Anderson, a story-teller, couldn't help going on with a story. From past experience with Anderson, Perkins knew what had happened. Last night after we had gone home, Anderson, lying awake, would have wished he had raised the subject of Hemingway's Catholicism; in his imagination he had heard himself raise certain questions; he had heard me answer; absorbed in his dream he had supplied a brilliant defense for me. In this extension of the real conversation, the thing that should have happened, would have happened; in his imagination it would have belonged completely to the small thing that did happen, and so it had truth for him.

Now Hemingway in his turn loved boxing. Every chance he got he must have boxed with someone, and he had all the lingo, he had hung around gyms, he had watched fighters at work. Something within him drove him to want to be expert at every occupation he touched. In those days he liked telling a man how to do things, but not by way of boasting or arrogance—it was almost as if he had to feel he had a sense of professionalism about every field of human behavior that interested him. To this day I know you will find some Broadway columnist, or some gym instructor in New York, who will assure the world he had seen Hemingway working out like a pro, or taking a punch at someone. The truth was that we were two amateur boxers. The difference between us was that he had given time and imagination to boxing; I had actually worked out a lot with good fast college boxers.

In Paris there were scoffers, envious men, always belittling Ernest, who would whisper that his physical roughness was all a bluff. It was utter nonsense. He was a big rough tough clumsy unscientific man. In a small bar, or in an alley, where he could have cornered me in a rough-and-tumble brawl, he might have broken my back, he was so much bigger. But with gloves on and in a space big enough for me to move around, I could be confident. My wife remembers how, when I came home, she would complain that my shoulders were black and blue. Laughing, I would explain that she should feel thankful; the shoulder welts and bruises meant Ernest had always missed my jaw or nose or mouth. She worried about the day coming when I would walk in with welts on my jaw or cheeks rather than my shoulders.

One dark cloudy afternoon I had called for Ernest and when we came out to the street, a soft rain had begun to fall. It was one of those lovely soft early-summer Paris rains. I was coatless; Ernest had brought a raincoat. We could have got a taxi, but the rain now was so gentle and the air so soft he said, "Let's walk." Taking one arm of the raincoat, he held that side of the coat out wide like a tent over me, his arm like a tent pole, and we loafed along. We talked. No big talk. Just gossip. It was like times at home at college when I might have called for an old friend and decided to walk with him in the rain because I liked being with him and felt sure of him.

That day, and for the first time, he did something that astonished me. At the American Club, we had undressed and got down to the business of boxing. By this time, knowing his style, I had worked out a routine. Moving in and out, I had to make him lead at me. He knew what I was doing. His brown eyes always on me, he waited for a chance to nail me solidly. When he finally threw his long left, I slipped it and then stepped in and caught him on the mouth with my own left. He knew by the book he should catch me with his right. It must have been exasperating to him that my left was always beating him to the punch. His mouth began to bleed. It had happened before. It wasn't important. His tongue kept curling along his lip, wiping off blood. Again he got hit on the lip, yet his eyes held mine as he swallowed the blood. But his mouth kept on bleeding. He loudly sucked in all the blood. He waited, watching me, and took another punch on the mouth. Then as I went to slip in again, he stiffened. Suddenly he spat at me; he spat a mouthful of blood; he spat in my face. My gym shirt too was spattered with blood.

I was so shocked I dropped my gloves. My face must have gone white, for I was shaken and didn't know what to do. It is a terrible insult for a man to spit at another man. We stared at each other. "That's what the bullfighters do when they're wounded. It's a way of showing contempt," he said solemnly.

My sense of outrage was weakened by my bewilderment when he suddenly smiled. Apparently he felt as friendly as ever. I tried to laugh. But we had to stop boxing so I could wipe off the blood. I didn't even complain, for I saw that he had more complete goodwill for me than ever. But I was wondering out of what strange nocturnal depths of his mind had come the barbarous gesture. What other wild gesture might he make in some dark moment in his life to satisfy himself, or put himself in a certain light, following, or trying to follow, some view he had of himself? But here he was, so sweet and likable again, so much at ease with me. I tried to tell myself he had put it just right; he had yielded to his boy-ish weakness for amusing and theatrical gestures. The whole thing could have been pure theatre.

As we sat down to talk before we dressed he seemed to be full of lighthearted enthusiasm. Standing up, he regarded me with a professional eye. "You're really a light heavy-weight," he insisted. "It's the way you're built. I thought at first it was just fat on you." I assented to this rather reluc-tantly, knowing I was twenty-five pounds overweight, simply potbellied and secretly ashamed of it. I liked eating. Then he told me he had written to Max Perkins, trying to describe the fun we had been having and my peculiar boxing style.

He suggested we go up to the Falstaff, off Montparnasse, an oak-paneled English bar presided over by Jimmy, a friend of his, an Englishman who had been a pro lightweight fighter. At that hour hardly anyone else was in the bar. Behind the bar Jimmy now looked like an amiable roly-poly host. Just a day or two ago I had been asking Jimmy what Lady Duff, the Lady Brett of *The Sun Also Rises*, was really like. Leaning across the bar, Jimmy had said confidentially, "You won't tell Hemingway, will you? No? Well, she was one of those horsey English girls with her hair cut short and the English manner. Hemingway thought she had class. He used to go dancing with her over on the Right Bank. I could never see what he saw in her."

But now Jimmy, observing the bag with the boxing gloves Ernest was carrying, and our scrubbed, wet-haired look, the look of men who have been exercising then showering, grinned knowingly. "You've been boxing, eh?" Smiling happily, Ernest touched his swollen lip, rolling it back to show it to Jimmy, the old fighter. I remember Ernest's line: "As long as Morley can keep cutting my mouth he'll always remain my good friend." We all laughed. Yet Ernest did look remarkably happy. His cut and swollen mouth seemed to make him feel jolly and talkative. He told how good Jimmy had been in the ring. He insisted Jimmy have a drink with with us. And the strange part of it was that in spite of the fact that Ernest had spat his blood on my face, I felt closer than ever to him.

But the look on his face as he spat at me must have stayed in my head. Of course I had to explain to Loretto the cause of the blood marks on my gym shirt. We wondered at the source of his unbridled impulse, so primitive and insulting. Supposing it had enraged me and caused us to part forever? Had such a thought ever entered his head?

Late one night we were at the Sélect, six or seven of us around two tables, and a pretty woman named Mary Bryant, whom I had never met before and who had been the wife of William Bullitt, the U.S. Ambassador to Moscow, told a story about Hemingway. She had had a Turkish boy as a protégé. This boy was an expert knife thrower. The boy had had been with her one time when she had told Hemingway he could throw a knife at twenty paces and pin an object, a man's hand for example, to a door. Getting up suddenly, Hemingway had gone over to the door, and thrust out his hand. "Come on, show me. Come on," he challenged the boy. "Pin my hand to the door." The story may or may not have been true. I had been rejecting all stories about Ernest that made him a strange dark primitive nocturnal figure. Yet now I seemed to know from what had happened between us that any time he faced a situation from which he ought to recoil protestingly or normally, he might start to play around with the destructive idea, testing his own courage in his imagination. In those days, as I said before, it seemed to me he could make the imagined challenging fear become so real, it might become unbearable. And he would act. Somehow these thoughts seem to tie up with that picture I had of him spitting the blood at me with such theatrical scorn, and then, knowing he shouldn't have done it, laughing.

At the Sélect that night, after hearing the story about the Turkish boy, I laughed with the others. Ernest did a lot of things that were merely imaginative gestures, I said. But they were only gestures. And I told about him spitting a mouthful of blood all over me when we were boxing, and how it hadn't altered our relationship at all. It was the only time I had talked about any incident in our boxing matches. Later on it became important to me to recall this one occasion. But the Quarter in those days, crowded as it was at certain hours with tourists, was a very small, backbiting, gossipy little neighborhood.

Morley Callaghan

Ford Madox
Ford

Brown Brothers

Ezra Pound

Brown Brothers

Sherwood
Anderson

Brown Brothers

Michael Arlen

Brown Brothers

LORETTO
CALLAGHAN

SINCLAIR LEWIS

Brown Brothers

MAXWELL PERKINS

Brown Brothers

ERNEST HEMINGWAY

F. Scott Fitzgerald

Brown Brothers

SYLVIA BEACH
AND
JAMES JOYCE

CHAPTER XVI

The Quarter was like a small town. It had little points of protocol, little indignities not to be suffered. There was a general awareness of what was going on in everyone else's life, a routine to be followed if the café was to be the center of your social life. For the Joyces or Gertrude Stein, the café was not the place where one entertained one's friends, or the place where wives showed up to meet their husbands. Nor did the Fitzgeralds, as we were to discover, belong to the Left Bank café set. But for us, not having the family responsibilities of the Hemingways and the Fitzgeralds, the late hours at the café were a happy time—unless a neighborhood indignity was being endured by a friend.

We had a friend, a middle-aged man named Edward Titus, who was the husband of Helena Rubenstein, the rich beautician. He lived by himself in a comfortable apartment

just around the corner at 4 rue Delambre. He was a famous
book collector and the publisher of the Black Maniken Press.
An agreeable quiet man, with graying hair combed straight
back, he had grown tired of the opulent display, the chauf-
feurs, and all the business detail that took up his time in the
great cosmetic firm of Helena Rubenstein. He had chucked
it all. He was living his own life. When the editor of the magazine *This Quarter* had died, Titus, not wanting the magazine to die too, had taken it over.

At nine thirty in the evening, Loretto and I would come
along the boulevard to the Sélect. Within half an hour Titus
would join us. Sometimes Helena Rubenstein would come
over to the Quarter from the Right Bank. She came to the
parties with a tall dark opera singer named d'Alvarez, who
wore evening dresses showing a broad and fascinating ex-
panse of bare back. Sometimes Madame Rubenstein would
come to the café with Titus, and he would have her sit with
us. In those days she was a very busy woman, growing stout,
but still dark, handsome and full of energy. Too much energy, I suppose, for sometimes she gave the impression of
wanting to take a little nap. When she was with us there was
always an amusing interplay about paying for the saucers.
Titus was an old resident of the Quarter; no one treated him
as a visiting businessman who was expected to pay the shot,
and he seemed to know that if he ever gave in and picked up
the tab just because he was rich, he would lose all caste with
the people whose respect he wanted. Quite properly he paid
for his own saucers as I for mine.

At the end of an evening Helena Rubenstein would watch,
aloof and impatient, while the waiter busily counted up our
separate piles of saucers. "Pay for them, Edward," she would
say imperiously. Did she ever understand his reluctance? I

wonder. Maybe she didn't care. As a grand dame, a figure of opulence, she could hardly sit there listening to the public bookkeeping. One way or another, only a couple of dollars was involved. Whenever she intervened, Titus understood that protocol was being broken; he was being made to look like an alien in the Quarter, and he didn't like it.

Though he was established in the neighborhood, and a publisher in his own right, Titus did not know Joyce, Pound, Wyndham Lewis, Hemingway, Fitzgerald or McAlmon. It was hard to explain why he didn't know any of these people. I used to wonder if there was a lot of anti-Semitism in the Quarter.

McAlmon, having returned to Paris, had quickly looked us up. I liked McAlmon. No matter what they say about him, his judgment of other writers was respected by some of the best people on earth. His destructive malice didn't bother me at all. If a man of talent was in any kind of trouble, McAlmon would help him if he could.

When he met my wife, he showed he was pleased with her; then he had to jab his little needle into me, or her, and sow the seeds of discord. "You had me fooled," he said to her some hours after meeting us. "I thought you were Spanish. You're Irish." And then he added with a touch of weary disdain, "You ought to be always dressed well, be seen in *Vogue* and *Harper's Bazaar*. It's too bad. Morley won't bother. You might as well know it now." When he saw we were laughing at him, he didn't mind; he laughed too.

I had asked Titus if he would like to meet McAlmon. Indeed he would, he said. That night McAlmon came to the Sélect.

Alone with me, or even when my wife was along, McAlmon never behaved badly, or got outrageously drunk. Maybe

he felt ill at ease with Titus, or wasn't sure how he felt about
him, therefore he had to drink a lot very quickly. I had asked
if he had heard whether Fitzgerald was in Paris. It set him
off. He told of a meeting with the Fitzgeralds when Zelda
had cast a lustful eye at him. Titus, who had said little, and
no wonder, pricked up his ears. I laughed cynically and shook
my head at Titus. When Bob McAlmon had had a drink or
two he seemed to believe every good-looking citizen, man
or woman, postman or countess, wanted to make a pass at
him.

Along the street came those two willowy graceful young
men from Montreal whom McAlmon called affectionately
"the clever little devils." Sauntering into the café with their
bland and distinguished air, they saw us and bowed. My
lighthearted wave of the hand piqued McAlmon. "Oh, you
don't understand those two at all," he jeered. But I did understand that the two boys shared his snickering wit. Friends
of his they might be, but it didn't stop them from laughing
at him. Just before his return, his Contact Press had printed
one of his own poems. One boy would look at the other solemnly, quote a line from the poem, "Is this the Aztec heart
that writhes upon the temple floor," then they would both
kill themselves laughing.

His view of the boys amused me and I said so. We kept
jibing and jeering at each other, offering contrasting views of
the boys. Titus, brightening and becoming an alert editor,
suggested we should both write stories; he would publish the
two stories side by side in the next issue of *This Quarter*.
Immediately I agreed to do it. So did McAlmon.

By the way, I did write the story, "Now That April's
Here," and Titus did publish it. Ezra Pound wrote me a letter from Rapallo expressing his admiration of the story and

suggesting that I go to Washington and write about the politicians in the same manner.

By now McAlmon, exhilarated by our debate, and getting tight, had become truly expansive. He ordered another champagne cocktail and a Welsh rarebit. When the waiter brought the rarebit McAlmon tasted it, and dropped his fork. "Tell Madame Sélect," he said in a disgusted tone, "that this rarebit did not come from the kitchen. It came from the toilet." The waiter hurried to Madame Sélect.

She was a plump, dark, determined-looking woman with a round high-colored face, who watched over the cash register and the waiters. Indeed she was the café boss. Approaching our table, quivering with rage, she told McAlmon she, herself, had made the rarebit. In that case, said McAlmon, waving his hand disdainfully, she ought to know where it came from. Aghast, she snatched the plate off the table and fled to the kitchen. In a little while she came out and stood back from the terrace at the door, watching us balefully, muttering, throwing glances of hatred at McAlmon, who had kept on laughing.

McAlmon's real target, and I couldn't put it past him if he was in one of his contemptuous moods, may have been Titus. Half drunk as he was, did he feel compelled to show some disrespect to this other publisher whose aims were so different from his own? In the meantime I had turned to watch a group of young homosexuals two tables away. The expression on my face must have irritated McAlmon. Maybe I did look too concerned. Four of the young homosexuals were commiserating with a sad-looking young fellow of twenty-five, whose story we knew. His wife, now on her way from the States to join him, did not know that in the months he had been without her, he had been corrupted by these boys. Now he had no desire to see her. McAlmon, evidently resenting my expression of concern or pity, wanted to offend me. Knowing I had kept all my good feeling for Hemingway, he struck very deftly at him. In *The Sun Also Rises,* why had Hemingway treated these homosexuals in such a vulgar orthodox manner? he asked. The answer was simple: he had been catering to all the virile men of the Middle West. All he had been really doing was strutting and flexing his own big powerful muscles, asserting his own virility—something, said McAlmon, looking down his nose, that was open to question. "So, Morley old boy, don't you start turning up your nose at homosexuals," he said, "or I'll suspect you too."

"It's the one boy there, Bob. I feel sorry for him."

"You're ridiculous," he said, and he began a funny, mocking, eloquent, but often loud defense of homosexuals. As Titus showed his embarrassment, McAlmon went on talking grandly about Plato and Michelangelo. Our objections only aroused his chuckling disdain. He was happily drunk. Suddenly he cried exuberantly, "I'm bisexual myself, like Michelangelo, and I don't give a damn who knows it." He hurled his glass out to the sidewalk where it splintered in front of an elderly man who stopped, rattled, waving his hand as if he were calling the police.

Madame Sélect, who had been standing at her post, watching and scowling at McAlmon and brooding over the insult to her rarebit, now came rushing over to the table. McAlmon would pay for the glass, she cried. Not only would he pay, she added grimly, he would leave the café at once. With a patient, tolerant smile, McAlmon rose, tried to bow, then had to sit down quickly—he couldn't move. While he sat there staring earnestly at the table top, his face chalk white, I went for a taxi. When I returned, Titus told me Madame

Sélect had said my friend was not welcome at her café any more.

Glancing at Madame Sélect, who waited, her arms folded, grim, solid and unyielding, Titus urged me to hurry and get McAlmon into a taxi. I did. But again for Titus, the protocol was broken; being treated as a businessman, he was left paying for McAlmon's drinks, the Welsh rarebit, the broken glass, and our drinks too. Though McAlmon, in the taxi, was in a stupor, as I looked at him I wondered if he hadn't actually wanted this to happen.

Now a matter of the greatest dignity began to concern our little neighborhood. Next night at nine thirty when Loretto and I came along the boulevard, Titus, in his chair at the Sélect, stood up and beckoned. We bowed apologetically. We went to a new little café between the Rotonde and the Sélect. Each night we followed this procedure. From his chair at the Sélect, Titus could see us sitting at the new place. We hated this little café. No one we knew sat there. Sometimes one of our friends, feeling sympathy for the grandeur of our position—the support of a drunken friend— would come and sit with us.

Each night Titus watched us with a lonely and disgusted expression on his face. Sometimes we saw him arguing with Madame Sélect. They would both grow vehement. One night, after they had had one of these cold grim arguments, we saw Madame Sélect and her headwaiter come out to the sidewalk, look along to the café where we sat, and contemplate us in silence.

It went on like this all week. On Saturday night as we were passing the Sélect at nine thirty, Titus came hurrying from his place on the terrace. "Madame Sélect would like a word with you," he said coaxingly and he beckoned to her.

We waited, aloof, dignified, beyond reproach as she came toward us, all grace, smiles and kindly benevolence. Would we sit down and have a drink on her? she asked. Would we invite our friend McAlmon to come and have a drink on her? There was much handshaking all around and so we sat down at the Sélect again, confident that a great victory for something or other had been won.

CHAPTER XVII

On the boulevard one night at the *apéritif* hour we encountered McAlmon. "What are you doing tonight?" he asked.

"Nothing, as usual."

"I'm having dinner with Jimmy Joyce and his wife at the Trianon. Why don't you join us?"

Jimmy Joyce! "No," I said quickly. "I understand he hates being with strangers and won't talk about anybody's work."

"Who told you all this?"

"Hemingway."

"Oh, nuts," he said, curling his lip. "Don't you want to see Jimmy? You'll like him. You'll like Nora, too."

"Well, of course we want to meet Joyce."

"See you in about an hour and a half at the Trianon," and he went on his way.

He had made it sound as if anyone could drop in on the

Joyces at any time. Jimmy, he had called him. Yet Sylvia Beach kept on throwing up her protective screen as dozens of English and American scholars tried to get close to the Irish master. What kind of magic touch did McAlmon have? Was it possible that Joyce had the same sneaking respect for McAlmon that I had myself and liked drinking with him? We'd soon see. At twilight we approached the Trianon just as casually as we might approach a bus stop.

It was a restaurant near the Gare Montparnasse, where the food was notably good. Just to the right as you go in we saw McAlmon sitting with the Joyces. The Irishman's picture was as familiar to us as any movie star's. He was a small-boned, dark Irishman with fine features. He had thick glasses and was wearing a neat dark suit. His courtly manner made it easy for us to sit down, and his wife, large bosomed with a good-natured face, offered us a massive motherly ease. They were both so unpretentious it became impossible for me to resort to Homeric formalities. I couldn't even say, "Sir, you are the greatest writer of our time," for Joyce immediately became too chatty, too full of little bits of conversation, altogether unlike the impression we had been given of him. His voice was soft and pleasant. His humor, to my surprise, depended on puns. Even in the little snips of conversation, he played with words lightly. However, none of his jokes made his wife laugh out loud, and I was reminded of McAlmon's story that she had once asked the author of the comic masterpiece *Ulysses,* "Jimmy, have we a book of Irish humor in the house?"

No matter what was being said, I remained aware of the deep-bosomed Nora Joyce. The food on the table, the white tablecloths, our own voices, everything in the restaurant seemed to tell me Joyce had got all the stuff of Molly Bloom's great and beautiful soliloquy at the close of *Ulysses* from this woman sitting across from me; all her secret, dark night thoughts and yearning. Becoming a little shy, I could hardly look at her. But the quiet handsome motherly woman's manner soon drove all this nonsense out of my head. She was as neighborly and sympathetic as Joyce himself. They both gossiped with a pleasant ease.

The sound of Joyce's voice suddenly touched a memory of home which moved me. My father, as I have said, didn't read modern prose, just poetry. Fond of music as he was, he wouldn't listen to jazz. He wouldn't read Anderson. I had assumed he would have no interest in experimental prose. When that copy of *This Quarter* carrying my first story, along with the work of Joyce, Pound, Stein, Hemingway and others, had come to our house, my father sat one night at the end of the kitchen table reading it. Soon he began to chuckle to himself. The assured little smirk on his face irritated me. Passing behind his shoulder, I glanced down at the page to see what he was reading. "Work In Progress," by James Joyce, which was a section from *Finnegan's Wake*. Imagining he was getting ready to make some sarcastic and belittling remark, I said grimly, "All right. What's so funny?"

But he looked up mildly; he had untroubled blue eyes; and he said with genuine pleasure, "I think I understand this. Read it like Irish brogue. . . . Shem is short for Shemus just as Jem is joky for Jacob. A few toughnecks are gettable. . . . It's like listening to someone talking in a broad Irish brogue, isn't it, Son?" "Yeah," I said. But I felt apologetic.

And now, after listening to Joyce in our general gossiping, I blurted out that my father had said the new Joyce work should be read aloud in an Irish brogue. Whether it was Joyce or McAlmon who cut in quickly, agreeing, I forget. It came out that Joyce had made some phonograph records of the work; in the way he used his voice it had been his intention to make you feel you were listening to the brogue; much of the music and meaning was in the sound of the broque. So my father had helped me; I wanted to go on: had Joyce read those proofs of *A Farewell to Arms* which I knew Hemingway had taken to him? Why not ask him? But there had been that warning from Hemingway, "He doesn't like to talk about the work of other writers." I felt hand-cuffed, exasperated, and therefore was silent. So Joyce had to make most of the conversation. Were we going to London? Sooner or later? He wrote down the name of an inexpensive hotel near the Euston Station.

McAlmon, who had been drinking a lot as usual, suddenly got up, excused himself and went toward the washroom. And then, almost as soon as McAlmon's back was turned, Joyce, leaning across the table, asked quietly, "What do you think of McAlmon's work?"

Surprised, I couldn't answer for a moment. Joyce? Someone else's work? Finally I said that McAlmon simply wouldn't take time with his work; he had hypnotized himself into believing the main thing was to get down the record.

"He has a talent," Joyce said. "A real talent; but it is a disorganized talent." And as he whispered quickly about this disorganized talent, trying to get it all in before McAlmon could return, I wanted to laugh. How had the story got around that the man wouldn't talk about another writer? Then Joyce suddenly paused, his eyes shifting away. McAlmon was on his way back from the washroom and like a conspirator Joyce quickly changed the subject.

As McAlmon came sauntering over to us with his superior air, I noticed a change in his appearance. He looked as if he had just washed his face and combed his hair. From past experience I knew what it meant. When with people he respected he would not let himself get incoherently drunk; he would go to the washroom; there he would put his finger down his throat, vomit, then wash his face, comb his hair and return sober as an undertaker.

It was now about ten o'clock. Turning to his wife, Joyce used the words I remember so well. "Have we still got that bottle of whiskey in the house, Nora?"

"Yes, we have," she said.

"Perhaps Mr. and Mrs. Callaghan would like to drink it with us."

Would we? My wife said we would indeed and I hid my excitement and elation. An evening at home with the Joyces, and Joyce willing to talk and gossip about other writers while we killed a bottle! Stories about Yeats, opinions about Proust! What would he say about Lawrence? Of Hemingway? Did he know Fitzgerald's work? It all danced wildly in my head as we left the restaurant.

Looking for a taxi, McAlmon had gone ahead with Mrs. Joyce and Loretto. Joyce and I were trailing them. The street was not lighted very brightly. Carried away by the excitement I felt at having him walking beside me, I began to talk rapidly. Not a word came from him. I thought he was absorbed in what I was saying. Then far back of me I heard the anxious pounding of his cane on the cobblestones and turned. In the shadows he was groping his way toward me. I had forgotten he could hardly see. Then headlights of an approaching taxi picked him up, and in the glaring light he waved his stick wildly. Conscience-stricken, I wanted to cry out. Rushing back, I grabbed him by the arm as the taxi swerved around us. I stammered out an apology. He made some pun on one of the words I used. I don't remember the pun, but since I was trembling the poor quick pun seemed to make the situation Joycean and ridiculous.

The Joyces lived in a solid apartment house, and in the entrance hall Mrs. Joyce explained we would have to use the lift in shifts; it was not supposed to carry more than two people at one time. For the first ascension my wife and Mrs. Joyce got into the lift. When it returned, McAlmon offered to wait while Joyce and I ascended. No, said Joyce, the three of us would get in. The lift rose so slowly I held my breath. No one spoke. Out of the long silence, with the three of us jammed together, came a little snicker from Joyce. "Think what a loss to English literature if the lift falls and the three of us are killed," he said dryly.

The Joyce apartment, at least the living room in which we sat, upset me. Nothing looked right. In the whole world there wasn't a more original writer than Joyce, the exotic in the English language. In the work he had on hand he was exploring the language of the dream world. In this room where he led his daily life I must have expected to see some of the marks of his wild imagination. Yet the place was conservatively respectable. I was too young to have discovered then that men with the most daringly original minds are rarely eccentric in their clothes and their living quarters. This room was all in a conventional middle-class pattern with, if I remember, a brown-patterned wallpaper, a mantel, and a painting of Joyce's father hanging over the fireplace. Mrs. Joyce had promptly brought out the bottle of Scotch. As we began to drink, we joked and laughed and Joyce got talking about the movies. A number of times a week he went to the movies. Movies interested him. As he talked, I seemed to see him in a darkened theatre, the great prose master absorbed in camera technique, so like the dream technique, one picture then another flashing in the mind. Did it all add to his knowledge of the logic of the dream world?

As the conversation began to trail off, I got ready. At the right moment I would plunge in and question him about his contemporaries. But damn it all, I was too slow. Something said about the movies had reminded McAlmon of his grandmother. In a warm, genial, expansive mood, and as much at home with the Joyces as he was with us, he talked about his dear old grandmother, with a happy nostalgic smile. The rich pleasure he got out of his boyhood recollections was so pure that neither the Joyces nor my wife nor I could bear to interrupt. At least not at first. But he kept it up. For half an hour he went on and on. Under my breath I cursed him again and again. Instead of listening to Joyce, I was listening to McAlmon chuckling away about his grandmother. Quivering with impatience I looked at Joyce, who had an amused little smile. No one could interrupt McAlmon. Mrs. Joyce seemed to have an extraordinary capacity for sitting motionless and looking interested. The day would come, I thought bitterly, when I would be able to tell my children I had sat one night with Joyce listening to McAlmon talking about his grandmother.

But when McAlmon paused to take another drink, Joyce caught him off balance. "Do you think Mr. and Mrs. Callaghan would like to hear the record?" he asked his wife.

"What record?" asked McAlmon, blinking suspiciously, and for a moment I, too, thought Joyce had been referring to him. Now Mrs. Joyce was regarding my wife and me very gravely. "Yes," she said. "I think it might interest them."

"What record?" McAlmon repeated uneasily.

Mrs. Joyce rose, got a record out of a cabinet and put it on the machine. After a moment my wife and I looked at each other in astonishment. Aimee Semple McPherson was preaching a sermon! At that time everyone in Europe and America had heard of Mrs. McPherson, the attractive, seductive blond evangelist from California. But why should Joyce be interested in the woman evangelist? and us? and McAlmon? Cut off, and therefore crestfallen, he, too, waited, mystified. Joyce had nodded to me, inviting my scholarly attention. And Mrs. Joyce, having sat down, was watching my wife with a kind of saintly concern.

The evangelist had an extraordinary voice, warm, low, throaty and imploring. But what was she asking for? As we listened, my wife and I exchanging glances, we became aware that the Joyces were watching us intently, while Mrs. McPherson's voice rose and fell. The voice, in a tone of ecstatic abandonment, took on an ancient familiar rhythm. It became like a woman's urgent love moan as she begged, "Come, come on to me. Come, come on to me. And I will give you rest . . . and I will give you rest. . . . Come, come. . . ." My wife, her eyebrows raised, caught my glance, then we averted our eyes, as if afraid the Joyces would know what we were thinking. But Joyce, who had been watching us so attentively, had caught our glance. It was enough. He brightened and chuckled. Then Mrs. Joyce, who had also kept her eyes on us, burst out laughing herself. Nothing had to be explained. Grinning mischievously, in enormous satisfaction with his small success, Joyce poured us another drink.

Before we could comment his daughter, a pretty, dark young woman, came in. And a few minutes later, his son too joined us. It was time for us to leave.

When we had taken Robert McAlmon, publisher of the city of Paris, home, we wandered over to the Coupole. That night we shared an extraordinary elation at being in Paris. We didn't want to go back to the apartment. In the Coupole bar we met some friends. One of them asked Loretto if she could do the Charleston. There in the bar she gave a fine solo performance. A young, fair man, a Servian count, who had been sitting at the bar holding a single long-stemmed red rose in his hand, had been watching her appreciatively. But one of our friends told him the dancing girl was my wife. With a shy, yet gallant bow to me from a distance, he asked if he had permission to give Loretto the rose. It was a good night.

CHAPTER XVIII

But the day and night I always remember came a week later. The May weather was so fine I didn't want to stay in the apartment in the afternoons and work. Bit by bit, looking at paintings had become part of our daily fare. Everybody in Paris seemed to paint, and in store windows in strange little streets you would see reproductions of Matisse, Derain, Rouault, Chirico, Modegliani, Picasso, Utrillo, and in the Quarter the surrealists Picabia and Miró were famous names. At that time there was still a common language of painting; the language hadn't got broken up. The painters hadn't quite entered their tower of Babel.

Some writers like to sit for long hours at their desks. Not me. At that time the *New Yorker* had written asking if I had any stories. I began to work on some. And I was also working on the novel that was to be called *It's Never Over*. But the

Paris streets were my workshop. While loafing along the streets ideas for the stories would grow in my head. Little street scenes would seem to distract me, would indeed get my full attention: the intent expression on the faces of men hurrying to the street urinals; workingmen quarreling under the eyes of a gendarme, each seeking the triumph of provoking the other to strike the first blow and get arrested. Or some little street whore would make me wonder, "Why are so many of these girls of the same short solid build as the whores Lautrec loved to paint?" A writer is always working. I can remember watching the ease and style with which Lacoste and Cochet handled Big Bill Tilden in the Davis Cup tennis matches and telling myself it had something to do with style in writing. When I got back to the apartment I would sit by the window overlooking the prison wall and write rapidly, most of the work having been done in my head before I came home. Often it rained. It was the time for reading. Very late at night was also a good time. From the window I could watch the bicycle patrol, the three tough French cops no one wanted to tangle with, come peddling slowly down the street.

Even when reading a writer is busily at work watching how an effect is achieved on the page. But whether I was reading D. H. Lawrence or Tolstoi or Virginia Woolf I would notice that when I hit certain scenes I would be so carried away I would cease to be aware of style or method. What then made good writing good? That was always the question. Freshness? Verbal felicity? No, there always seemed to be some other quality. There had been at the time a quarrel about the methods of Arnold Bennett and Virginia Woolf; Bennett's or Zola's camera eye and Virginia Woolf's interior flow of impressions. But it seemed to me, reading so late at night in my room overlooking the prison wall, that there could be no quarrel at all. The temperament, the character, the very identity of the writer was in his kind of eye. Virginia Woolf had a sensibility so fragile it must have been always close to the breaking point; she couldn't have written any other way. And Lawrence? Again the writer's own character gave his work its identity. He must have been an Anglo-Saxon puritan with an inborn uneasiness about female flesh; he must have hated this uneasiness, and hungered for the expression of ecstasy; therefore the natural poetry of sex. But then I would wonder why Lady Chatterley's correct copulations didn't move me as much as one surrender by Anna Karenina, or one of poor Emma Bovary's fugitive rolls in the hay.

At the cafés, of course, one could always get an argument on these questions. But I knew what I was seeking in my Paris street walks, and in the typing hours—with Loretto waiting to retype a chapter. It was this: strip the language, and make the style, the method, all the psychological ramifications, the ambience of the relationships, all the one thing, so the reader couldn't make separations. Cézanne's apples. The appleness of apples. Yet just apples.

Wandering around Paris I would find myself thinking of the way Matisse looked at the world around him and find myself growing enchanted. A pumpkin, a fence, a girl, a pineapple on a tablecloth—the thing seen freshly in a pattern that was a gay celebration of things as they were. Why couldn't all people have the eyes and the heart that would give them this happy acceptance of reality? The word made flesh. The terrible vanity of the artist who wanted the word without the flesh. I can see now that I was busily rejecting even then that arrogance of the spirit, that fantasy running through modern letters and thought that man was alien in this universe. From Pascal to Henry Miller they are the children of St. Paul.

Often we would go to the Luxembourg Museum and then, when tired, sit in the gardens and watch the little girls in their severe black frocks sailing their boats on the pond. On this particular day we had spent hours in those galleries on the rue Bonaparte. We had eaten at a small café down that way. It was dark when we wandered up to Montparnasse. Sitting at the café I had got to thinking about Fitzgerald. Until then we had counted on Hemingway letting us know if he had news of the Fitzgeralds. But what if they were in Paris and hadn't as yet got in touch with Ernest? I had a hunch it was time to go looking for them ourselves.

The hour was about nine thirty, and as we saw it, a reasonable hour to go calling. If the Fitzgeralds had been out for dinner, well, by this time they might be home. And Max Perkins had said, "Don't write to Scott. Don't be formal. Just drop in on him."

The Fitzgeralds lived near the St. Sulpice Cathedral in an old stone building which must have been a great house at one time. As soon as we got out of the taxi I said to Loretto, "Why, this place isn't more than a stone's throw from Hemingway's place. Or at least a stone thrown twice." It was a fact I was to remember later and brood on. Standing in the little vestibule, we scanned the apartment nameplates. There, indeed, was the Fitzgerald name. We rang the bell. No one answered. As we turned away disappointed, at loose ends standing in the shadowed doorway, a taxi drew up. A man and woman got out. They were under a streetlight. We could see their faces. "Why, there's Fitzgerald," I said to Loretto. In that light, even from a distance, he looked like the handsome, slender, fine-featured man whose picture I had so often seen, whose profile, in fact, appeared to be copied again and again by magazine illustrators. Coming toward us slowly, they couldn't see us. We were half hidden in the shadows. The vestibule light touched Zelda's blond hair. A handsome woman, her features were as regular as Scott's. I don't know why it upset me seeing these fine classic heads coming into the vestibule shadows where we waited.

Stepping out I said, "I'm Morley Callaghan and this is Loretto." Startled for a moment, they had no words for us. They seemed to be trying to get used to the sight of us on their doorstep. "Well, hello, how are you?" Scott said. Then, half confused, he added, "Why didn't you let us know you were in Paris?" We all shook hands. Opening the door he led us in.

His manner was correctly courteous. All the little gentlemanly amenities seemed to be important to him. There was nothing lazy or slovenly about his speech or his movements. His light brown hair was cut cleanly and combed exactly, and he spoke with a quiet precise firmness. He was slender and of medium height. In the cut of his jaw, in his little gestures, there was a forcefulness, almost a sense of authority. Perhaps it was the manner of a man who knew he should always appear in this light; yet he did seem to assert a deep confidence in his own importance. It was attractive and somehow reassuring. Later on it came out that this sense of his importance both sustained and tormented him. Yet meeting him there for the first time I can see now that if he had been told that night that he would become the Phoenix of modern letters he would not have been surprised. A proud man, he would have taken it as his due. And his wife too had the appearance, I say the appearance, of this strange confidence. In her handsome face there was a firmness that was almost a stubbornness, a kind of challenging confidence that didn't put one quickly at ease with her, and yet made one believe in all the wild stories one had heard about her. They both looked as if they were cut from an expensive pattern that included the big apartment.

It was a big elegant apartment, a far more elaborate apartment than Hemingway's place, and whereas I could think of Hemingway's or Joyce's apartments as having living rooms, in this place of Scott's I knew I was in a drawing room. It had period furniture, too. We all sat down and looked at each other, not apprehensively or critically, just trying to get used to each other quickly. Then Scott explained that they had been to a theatrical performance, I forget whether it was ballet or a play. From what we had heard of Zelda we expected perhaps a grand gesture, a rippling laugh or some romantic absurdity. Instead, she sat with a little smile, studying us. They asked if we had seen the Hemingways. When we said indeed we had, Scott wanted to know when, and asked if we often saw Ernest. He got drinks for us. Then we all seemed to relax and grow animated, and I could see that Scott was a man of sudden quick enthusiasms who, after he had made up his mind that you were temperamentally akin to him, wasn't concerned about withholding anything of himself. I liked him immediately. In fact it was a joy to see that he was so much like the picture of him I had kept in my thoughts.

Soon we were talking about anything and everything, all getting a little closer to each other. Suddenly he asked if we had read *A Farewell to Arms*. Only some parts of it? Hurrying to his study he returned with a manuscript copy, and glowing with enthusiasm, he fumbled through the pages till he found the part he wanted. "Just listen to this," he said. He read that passage, "—if people bring so much courage to this world the world has to kill them to break them—" He read it with emotion. When he finished he asked quietly, "Isn't it beautiful?"

"Well, yes it is," I agreed, "but . . ." Maybe I frowned as I deliberated. It was hard to describe the impression the passage had made on me. Finally I said, "Of course it's beautiful, but . . ."

"But what?" Scott asked gravely.

"But maybe it's too deliberate. Maybe the rhythmic flow is too determined, and the passage emerges as a set piece."

Certainly it was lyrical, Scott said, shrugging and changing his tone, but for that matter the whole book was lyrical. He waited, watching me, then he shrugged. "All right, it doesn't impress you."

"If you ask me, it sounds pretty damned Biblical," Zelda said firmly. Perhaps she had heard the passage read to her many times. Anyway, she seemed to be relieved to have someone else on her side. "If you're not impressed, it's all right, Morley," Scott assured me. With an injured air he riffled through some more pages of the manuscript, then paused, pondered, came to some firm decision, closed the book, put it aside and sat listening as Zelda became talkative about prose generally. But even on that first night I became aware that Scott kept an eye on her. He let her talk on, saying little himself, just listening; then abruptly, to our surprise, he told her that she was tired. She did look tired. She should go to bed, he said firmly. Turning to us, he explained she was taking ballet lessons and had to get up early; he hoped we would understand. We didn't quite understand; she left either too meekly or too willingly.

We were left with Scott, who was sitting by himself about

eight feet away from us, regarding me too solemnly. Having poured himself another drink, he began to ask my opinion of some American writers. All my answers were frank. Making no comment, he kept on drinking, smiling encouragement. Then I became aware that he was nodding to himself, as if agreeing with himself, not with me. Leaning forward, his face suddenly pale, he said, "Let's have lunch tomorrow, Morley."

"I'd be glad to have lunch," I said. Perhaps I should have expressed more warmth and enthusiasm, but his tone and his pallor now worried me. The way he watched me began to make me feel unhappy.

"Whom would you like to have lunch with us?" he asked mildly, his head on one side.

"It doesn't matter, Scott."

"Clive Bell, the art critic, is in town. Do you know his work?"

"I've read his book."

"No," he said, pondering and still watching me intently. "No, I don't think he impresses you enough."

"I'd like to meet him, if you'd like to have him along," I said, laughing awkwardly. In a swift glance at my wife I saw she was as uneasy as I was. In our hurt embarrassment we both waited. Though Scott had an awful pallor, and I knew he was getting drunk, he smiled sweetly, his head on one side again, as he considered some grave problem. "No, I don't think Clive Bell impresses you, Morley," he said, with his deceptive smile. Then half to himself, "Who does impress you, Morley?"

My face began to burn, and my wife, stiffening, sat helplessly on the edge of her chair, no doubt remembering all I had told her about Scott. With her eyes she was pleading with me to go. But before I could speak, stand up, make the necessary polite little remarks, Scott himself stood up slowly. "Would this impress you, Morley?" he asked sweetly.

Suddenly he got down on his knees, put his head on the floor and tried to stand on his head. One leg came up, and he tried to get the other one up and maintain his balance. And while he was swaying and flopping at my feet, my shame and anger became unbearable. I thought of that afternoon on Fifth Avenue when I had walked up to the Plaza, wondering about him, moved by his generosity in going into Scribner's with my story, and how anxious I had been for his friendship. Now here he was on the floor of his own drawing room, trying to stand on his head to mock me. In my anger and anguish, I felt there must be some dreadful flaw in my character which he had immediately perceived. Then he lost his balance and sprawled flat on his face. I got up and helped him to his feet. "You're a little drunk," I said. "No, not at all," he said, and he was almost convincing, for as soon as he got to his feet he had good balance and control of himself. It was nice meeting him, we said. Untroubled, he walked us to the door and shook hands politely. We said good night.

Outside, heartbroken and humiliated, I walked along beside Loretto. "He was drunk, that's all," she said sympathetically. "Yet how did it happen to him so quickly?"

"Even if it was the alcohol," I said bitterly, "it only helped him to show what he thought of me."

Then Loretto stopped suddenly and turned to me, shaking her head in wonder. "Do you know you have the craziest friends?"

"Nobody else has been crazy."

"All along the way they've been crazy. Look. I met Sinclair

Lewis. What does this great man do? Puts on a first-class vaudeville act."

"He was very nice and you know it."

"He was wonderful. I loved him. And McAlmon?"

"He does crazy things, I admit."

"And the great Joyce plays an Aimee Semple McPherson record for a laugh. And Ernest? Imagine! He spits blood right in your face. It's insane."

"I like him and so do you."

"I like them all. They're all so attractive. All so wonderfully upsetting. How do I know what's going to happen next? We've just met a man we've always wanted to meet. What does he do? He doesn't spit. He stands on his head for us. Absolutely crazy too."

"Aren't you lucky?" I said. "I'm the only one who is calm, objective and rational."

CHAPTER XIX

As soon as I got up next day I wrote a letter to Scott. In the letter I asked him to forgive us for walking in on him un-announced—we shouldn't have done it. It would have been much more sensible to have written to him and informed him where we were in Paris, but Max Perkins had assured me that such a letter was unnecessary. If we had upset him and Zelda in any way, or if we had kept them up, we could only offer an apology.

A day later when I called for Hemingway, I told him what had happened. Smiling a little to himself as he listened, he offered neither advice nor consolation. What a gift he had for minding his own business and keeping his thoughts to himself. But he and Scott were supposed to be the best of friends. I was baffled. If I had asked his advice about a pub-lisher, an editor, a political situation or how to conduct myself in some activity requiring great physical skill, he would have been full of expert advice. All he said now was, "Well, that's Scott."

"Standing on his head!" I said bitterly. "It might have been better if I had punched him on the nose."

And I remember his odd smile as he shrugged. "There's no distinction in punching Scott on the nose," he said. "Every taxi driver in Paris has done it."

So Scott Fitzgerald, Ernest's friend, the figure I had built up in my imagination as my own good friend too, could go to the devil as far as I was concerned. I tried to put him out of my mind altogether. I told no one else around the Quarter about him. The day passed, and next afternoon Loretto and I went across the river to the American Express, then loafed around the Place Vendôme and the Madeleine. It was supposed to be Cocteau's neighborhood. We had seen photographs of his hands in so many store windows we joked about recognizing him on the street by his hands. The violent contrast between the elegant Frenchwomen coming out of the little shops and the black-stockinged plainly dressed working girls fascinated us.

That day, feeling restless, we wandered for hours from neighborhood to neighborhood. My wife had an extraordinary sense of direction. When we were lost we would agree to let her follow her nose, and sooner or later we would be on more familiar ground. I used to attribute her sure step to a little pair of brown shoes she wore. Anyway, that day after we had eaten, and got back to our apartment about eight, our carrot-topped plump Russian landlady stopped us in the hall. In her hopeless mixture of French and Russian, she tried to tell us a man and a woman had called. With her hands, her eyes, strange movements of her lips, a sway of her body and garbled words, she tried to describe our callers. The name? Did it sound like McAlmon? Mr. Hemingway? No. Well, we consoled her, it didn't matter. At the café later in the evening the friends would appear and find us at our table.

When we opened our door, there on the floor were three of those blue *pneumatiques,* the Paris special-delivery letters. We opened one. It was from Scott Fitzgerald. *Tried to see you after lunch,* he wrote, *but you were not at home.* The other two special-delivery letters told how he had kept looking for us. Speechless, we both sat down on the bed. Why had Scott come dashing back and forth after us? we wondered. I felt uneasy. Had my curt, cold note caused some kind of unpredictable trouble? If we, in our turn, sent him a special-delivery letter, I said, what was there to say? Was he the one who now felt insulted? Were we to have to explain how we had been injured? While we sat there a knock came on the door. Our Russian lady said, "Your friends . . ." I hurried to the door. Along the hall came Scott and Zelda, both with a breathless air. Without any aplomb at all we stared at them apprehensively. They weren't smiling. They were upset and determined. "Morley, I got your note," Scott blurted out. "This is terrible. All afternoon we've looked for you." He took me by the arm as my wife invited them in.

The concern in Scott's eyes, and the way Zelda was backing up this concern, overwhelmed us. Never in my life had anyone come to me so openly anxious to rectify a situation. They wouldn't sit down. Starting to make light of the whole situation, I faltered, knowing by the light in Scott's eyes that I would be belittling his generosity. He must have insisted that Zelda come with him; he must have carted her grimly around with him all afternoon, making her believe something very important to him was involved. I remember the expression on his face as I put out my hand, laughing; it had a curious kind of dignity, making me feel that he was the one, not I, who knew we ought to be better than we were. My wife told Zelda that she shouldn't have put herself to the trouble of coming after us; she was too generous. Then Scott, taking me by the arm again amid all our protestations of goodwill and self-depreciation, made one of those generous remarks which few other men could have made, and which seemed to come so easily out of his heart. "You see, Morley," he said simply, "there are too few of us."

His conduct of two nights before, my attitude, my hesitation about accepting the enchantment of that one passage in *A Farewell to Arms,* whatever it was that had set him off, making him feel I was hard to impress, was forgotten. Zelda said they couldn't sit down, they were on their way out for dinner and were late. On the way they had decided to make another try at catching up with us. Would we come to dinner with them tomorrow night? Would it be all right if we all sat at Joyce's table in the Trianon? They made us happy, we said. And Scott now believed us. We all shook hands warmly. They hurried out. We went to our window overlooking the Santé Prison wall, and as we watched the slim elegant Scott and his beautiful wife getting into the taxi they had kept waiting, I felt paradoxically both humble and important. What a charming man he was, said Loretto, moved as she watched the taxi pull away.

Next night at the appointed hour we met them at the Trianon. And indeed, just as he had promised, Scott said we were to sit at Joyce's table. But he led us to a table to the left, not the right side of the restaurant. We couldn't bear to tell him we had been there a few nights ago with Joyce. What did it matter that Joyce had been at another table? A man like Scott, talented as he was himself, got so much pleasure out of thinking he was at a master's table it would have been ridiculous to have said, "No, over there!" Now I can see that Scott at his best was lucky in his temperament. He was always being dazzled. The very rich—no, it would be fairer to say he was fascinated by the unlimited possibilities of action and enjoyment, a kind of possible grandeur of opulence offered by the enormously rich. Surely Balzac too was fascinated in the same way. To get the excitement of a schoolboy, sitting at Joyce's table! Well, Scott as much as anyone I ever met had a conception of an aristocracy of talent.

Even now I seem to hear Zelda's voice coming at us suddenly. "I write prose. It's good prose." Her strange intensity, the boldness of her insistence that she too be regarded as a talent, was surprising. She was leaning across the table, almost challenging me. What could I say except, "I'm sure it is"? She had had a story in *Scribner's* magazine which I had read. It was a story in a careful, determined style with a flash of metaphor.

And she was the one who first mentioned Hemingway. We had been talking about someone's manners. How odd that in those free-swinging, disorderly days in the Quarter there was so much awareness of a man's or a woman's manners! Zelda said, "Hemingway has charming manners, don't you think?" When we agreed she added, "He has the most charming manners of anyone I know."

Now it was plain that Ernest was more than a good writer to them. Scott had to have his heroes. Joyce was a hero, of course. But I wondered if he had made Ernest into a special kind of hero. Aside from his liking for him he seemed to believe Ernest had some capacity for the rich, adventurous experience that had been denied to him. Even there at "Joyce's table"—was our pretending somehow right in view of his attitude to Ernest?—as he asked me questions about him. I felt in him a yearning for closer friendship with the man. No, not friendship—rather comradeship. He asked when we had last seen Ernest and what we had done. I felt ridiculous, believing they were intimate friends. And with his strange candor he asked suddenly, "What do you make of Pauline? Do you find her attractive? Can you see her appeal for Ernest?" My wife and I agreed in saying simply that Pauline seemed to be a very nice woman.

But Scott began to weigh the matter. Yes, he could see that Ernest might find her attractive. But then he startled us. In his candid and intensely interested manner he said he had a theory about Ernest and his women. It was as if he had thought many times about Hemingway's divorce and remarriage and I can still hear him saying thoughtfully, "I have a theory that Ernest needs a new woman for each big book. There was one for the stories and *The Sun Also Rises*. Now there's Pauline. *A Farewell to Arms* is a big book. If there's another big book I think we'll find Ernest has another wife."

My wife and I looked at each other uncomfortably. If ever we should ask Ernest if he had a big new book in mind we would inevitably remember Scott's theory, wouldn't we? And Pauline? Could we ever ask about a new book in front of Pauline? But that theory of Scott's always remained in my mind. And over the years I had occasion to wonder if Scott didn't have far more insight into Ernest's temperament, as it was related to his work, than any of us.

By dinner's end we were laughing and at ease, and when we left the restaurant, just loafing along, all of Paris seemed to come a little closer. It was for me, as it had been for others for a thousand years, the place where the stranger could believe he was among his own people; the meeting place for all those who wanted to meet. As we walked along slowly in the moonlight, Zelda laughed out loud, looking around. She had the restless air, the little sway of a woman seeking some new exhilaration, a woman in Paris who knew the night should be just beginning. She kept saying, "What'll we do? Let's do something," and again she laughed. I remember her stopping suddenly on the street. "I know," she said. "Let's go roller skating."

The line has often come back to me, bringing the little street scene back vividly.

"Where do you go roller skating around here?" I asked.

"We can find a place. Don't you want to go roller skating, Loretto?"

"I'll go. I'm game."

"And you?" Zelda asked me.

"I've only roller skated two or three times," I said, half laughing. "I'll go along though, if you want to."

But Scott, who had been demurring politely, and who had, perhaps, counted on my saying I had no desire to roller skate, muttered impatiently the thing was to go no further. Suddenly he grabbed Zelda by the wrist. "I'm putting you into a taxi. You go home now and go to bed," he said. His peremptory tone on the shadowed street startled us. If I had grabbed my own wife by the wrist and told her I was putting her in a taxi, her eyes would have flashed; there would have been some kind of a struggle. Zelda's face was half hidden, yet her whole manner changed; it was as if she knew he had command over her; she agreed meekly. I could not know then that Zelda had begun to show many signs of her impending breakdown, and that Scott was having perhaps secret and painful difficulty with her. From the way she had spoken, her restless air on the street, Scott must have recognized some symptom. We were getting our first glimpse at the beginning of the tragedy of his life. Yet he had sounded so commanding; he did have this extraordinary authority over her. A taxi came along and he put her in it. And suddenly she had said good night like a small girl and was whisked away from us—and Scott dismissed the little scene almost brusquely.

"Zelda has to get up early in the morning. She's taking those ballet lessons," and he pointed out that girls as a rule started studying ballet when they were about twelve! Zelda had started when she was over thirty and it was hard for her; it was all very tiring. I asked him why she wanted to take up ballet dancing at her age. It was quite understandable, Scott said; she wanted to have something for herself, be something herself. I recalled her sudden aggressive assertion at dinner that she too was a good writer. Was she bent on competing with Scott for the limelight? Of course, that was it. How unlucky for Scott. And I remember taking Loretto's arm and looking at her, hoping she would never feel driven to jockey with me publicly for attention.

Scott was walking along with us, talking easily now as if nothing of particular interest had happened. He told us we really ought to visit the big cafés.

He suggested that we should walk along and sit at the Dôme. It was a place we ought to visit, he said. We wondered where he thought we had been all this time. Yet walking along to the Dôme, we held our peace. Why hadn't we told

him we had been in the Trianon with the Joyces, and now
that we sat every night at the Sélect near the Dôme? Because
of his eager enthusiasm, the pleasure he got out of offering
a new experience he thought would please you, I always had
the inclination when with him to keep quiet and not spoil
his fun. Sitting at the brightly lit Dôme terrace, so crowded
with tourists, he explained, like a man slumming, that the
Dôme had been just a little zinc bar. All the tourists were
there, he was sure, because they had read *The Sun Also
Rises*. I can still see him there on the terrace, all his wonderful availability in his quick conversation, his smile, his un-
spoilt eagerness to find goodwill and friendship in those he
liked. Then suddenly he asked, "Couldn't we all have dinner
together? Couldn't we get the Hemingways? Couldn't you
suggest it to Ernest, Morley?"

I certainly would suggest it, I agreed. We went on with
the conversation. Neighborhood characters were passing; our
drunken poet in his Pernod trance; the two bright boys with
that handsome girl who looked like a Turk; why did they
keep together even with her? Were they inseparable in
everything? But while I watched I was pondering over the
paradoxical relationships between men. I asked myself, Why
doesn't Scott speak to Ernest himself? Why pick on me? I
had been assuming that Scott was Ernest's intimate friend.
I did not feel that I was in the little circle of Hemingway's
close friends: there would have to be others he saw in Paris,
close old friends he would go to for companionship when
he was in trouble. Who these people were I didn't know. I
had thought that Scott for sure was one of them. What if
there wasn't such a group? How unlike the French writers
we were. Breton, Soupault, Aragon, Eluard, got together,
got excitement out of talking about writing. Sometimes I

had wondered if Ernest and I would see much of each other if we didn't go boxing. Who knows? Maybe Ernest didn't see much of anybody. Yet Scott, the devoted old friend, seemed to believe that I was the one Ernest was seeing. It was complicated. Perhaps Scott knew that Ernest now avoided the close friendship of other writers unless he had something in common with them aside from the writing. But like every man in the world who has a hero and imagines there is someone much closer to his hero than he is, Scott asked me to speak to Ernest and I was touched.

CHAPTER XX

It was in the back of my mind the next afternoon when I called for Ernest. He was waiting, and he had a friend with him, Joan Miró, the great Spanish surrealist painter. At that time Miró was at the beginning of his great international reputation. He looked to be about the same age as Ernest and he was small enough in stature to make me feel like a big man. He was about the size of Napoleon. He wore a neat dark business suit, and the kind of a shirt I hadn't seen for a long time; it had a stiffly starched front with stripes running crosswise. His hair was clipped close, and he had a quick warm smile and lively eager eyes. Unfortunately for me, he couldn't speak a word of English. Ernest said that Miró was coming with us to act as timekeeper. Miró beamed proudly. Outside, walking over to the American Club, we must have presented a strange spectacle: big Ernest over six feet and heavy, me, four or five inches shorter, and Miró, who might have been a little over five feet. Steps and stairs on the Paris street! And to make it a better picture, Miró not only had that stiff cross-stripes shirt, he wore one of those hard black bowler hats!

Taking advantage of the fact that Miró had no English, I told Ernest that Scott had called for us and we had dinner with him and Zelda and I now liked Scott very much. I remember the little conversation. About the proposition that we all get together he made no comment.

"You didn't tell Scott where I live, did you?" he said after a moment's reflection.

"No, I didn't."

"If you're going to be seeing a lot of Scott, don't tell him where we live, eh?"

"Why not? What's the matter?"

"The Fitzgeralds will come walking in on us at all hours."

"Can't you tell them there's a baby in the house? Tell them Pauline has to get some sleep."

"It won't stop them," and then he shrugged. "And besides, Zelda is crazy."

"How do you mean?"

"She's just crazy. You'll find out."

"Okay," I said.

At the time I thought he meant that Zelda wasn't predictable in the sense that Scott wasn't predictable either when a little drunk. Yet I felt troubled. A man as sensitive as Ernest would know beyond a doubt of Scott's admiration for him, and his liking too. Scott apparently had some need of the kind of close friendship he thought he could get from Ernest. It seemed to me Scott wanted to offer incredible loyalty to him. Look what had happened when Scott had believed I wasn't sufficiently impressed by that passage from *A Farewell to Arms*. Yet Ernest, for some reason I couldn't understand, some ridiculous scene between them, no doubt, or some series of irritations, or maybe because of some view he had of Scott and Scott's work, simply didn't want to be bothered with him. Yet they lived only a few blocks from each other. Scott didn't know it, and I was not to tell him.

Due, no doubt, to Miró's presence, it was one of our best boxing afternoons. At other times in our boxing Ernest and I would laugh and kid each other. Miró added a touch of solemn Spanish dignity to the affair. Taking off his neat coat, he carefully folded it. Moving with brusque efficiency, he studied his watch so he could call out accurately the beginning of the three-minute round and the minute rest. All his movements became precise, stern, polite and yet dominating. Never had I had a timekeeper so immersed in a match, and so commanding with his splendid dignified earnestness. To have laughed or not been workmanlike in our boxing would have been an insult to his dignity; he would have been disappointed in us. So it was a good afternoon. We were all happy and satisfied, and I thought that Miró, especially, had enjoyed himself.

Miró was having dinner with the Hemingways, but after the boxing I told them I was meeting Loretto at the Sélect. And here again was the charm of Hemingway. I didn't have to say to him, "Loretto, I know, would like to meet Miró." He simply said, "We'll walk up with you." When we got to the café there was Loretto, and Hemingway introduced Miró and they sat down with us for a few minutes.

I remember it was a dull gray day, but not dark enough to promise rain. Along the other side of the street passed those two boys, "the clever little devils," whom I had got to

like by this time. Their bland superiority and their awareness of what was going on in the Quarter was often amusing.
Now they sat down across the street at the Coupole. By the
way they were staring over at us I knew they had recognized Hemingway, whom they had never seen at the cafés.

"Did you read that 'Confessions of a Young Man' piece?"
I asked Ernest. The piece had appeared in *This Quarter*. It
must have been written when the boy was eighteen or nineteen. "Well, the fellow who wrote it," I said, "is sitting over
there looking at us."

"Which one?"

"The one on the right."

"It was a very funny piece," Hemingway said, laughing.
"You tell McAlmon that if he'll publish it I'll buy ten copies
to give to my friends."

When they were leaving, Miró picked up the bag containing the boxing gloves. He seemed to like carrying that bag.
They went slowly along the street, big Ernest, little Miró
in his bowler hat and neatly pressed dark suit, erect, precise
in his step.

When Miró and Ernest had got only fifty feet beyond the
café, the two boys, who had been watching carefully, came
hurrying across the street.

"Wasn't that Hemingway?" Graeme asked.

"Yes, that was Hemingway."

"And the other one," Buffy said blandly, watching the two
retreating figures. "His butler, I presume? Does he really
bring his butler along with him now to carry his bag?"

Their little snicker, in view of the picture Hemingway and
Miró made, was perfect. The remark indeed was bright. I let
them enjoy their mirth for a moment. Knowing I was going
to leave them feeling they had committed the most terrible

of sins around the Quarter, the sin of unawareness of what was going on, I said quietly, "No, that's Miró."

"Miró! The Spanish painter?"

"Yes. Not Hemingway's butler."

"Oh," and their faces fell, and they took a couple of quick steps out to the sidewalk so they could see the hard hat and the neat square shoulders of the little man carrying the bag, in an entirely different light. Then somewhat embarrassed, they sauntered away.

Sitting there by ourselves I told Loretto we had a situation on our hands; there was to be no getting together with the Hemingways and the Fitzgeralds. Ernest had warned me not to give Scott his address. Naturally we wondered, speculated, tried to come to some conclusion about who had put out the story that they were great and good friends. Come to think of it, I had never heard Ernest praise a book of Scott's. Yet Scott was still fiercely devoted to him. Was there something in Ernest's nature that made him want to slough off anyone who had affection for him? I wondered. On the other hand, aside from the impression I had got from Max Perkins, was there any evidence they had ever been as close as Scott wanted them to be?

"There's something about all this that doesn't make sense," Loretto said suddenly.

"What doesn't make sense?"

"Ernest doesn't see Scott because Scott is a drunk. Right?"

"And would upset his life and his work. That's right."

"But look, Morley. What about that manuscript copy of *Farewell to Arms* Scott showed us? Where would Scott get it?"

"Probably from Ernest."

"Exactly. Well, you don't go around handing out manuscripts to people you want to hide from, do you? So the decision that Scott is a nuisance must have been made pretty recently. A drunk! Are you sure that's all there is to it? You know it can't be. What goes on between them, anyway? Will Ernest ever tell us? Will Scott go on pretending he doesn't know?"

By this time Hemingway and Miró, far along the street, were just about out of sight, but I craned my neck, taking a last look at them. I was sure Scott would keep pushing away till he came along some afternoon with Ernest and me, came into that little area of interest and friendship that had nothing to do with our being writers.

CHAPTER XXI

At this time—it comes into my memory as being in the middle of the week—Loretto reminded me that the priest we had met on the boat, who had been so sure we would forget all about him, ought to be coming through Paris now on his return from his Mediterranean tour. That night we walked over to the Right Bank hotel, where we had parted from him on our first day in Paris. Since that first day, which now seemed so long ago, how rapidly the Quarter life had swirled around us.

The desk clerk said that indeed the priest's party did have a reservation at the hotel, a large touring party was booked into the hotel for the end of the week. We left a note for the priest—just our name and the address, and a few joking words—*I thought we were supposed to forget you.* Two days later, coming home after boxing, I heard voices in the apartment. Someone was laughing loudly. When I entered there was the priest with Loretto, and they were both laughing hilariously. On the floor were two champagne bottles. Other bottles were on a little table by the window. Jumping up, the priest embraced me. I was embarrassed by the warmth of his embrace and his emotion. No one could have called me his old and dear friend. My awkward laugh, my embarrassment, only made Loretto giggle. "He's just glad we were here," she said. "Just happy he knew someone in Paris." And Father Tom beamed at me.

Still giggling, she told me that his touring party had been made up of middle-aged Methodist women; in Italy they had watched him closely and disapprovingly; they had gossiped; furthermore they had been full of blue-nosed malice. And why? Because he had liked to consume the wine of the country. Every time he had sat down with them at dinner he could tell by their sly, knowing glances they had been gossiping about him. Whenever he went off on his own, they took their little digs at him. On his return they would practically smell his breath, convinced he would be reeking of liquor. He had wanted to express his contempt for them, yet couldn't. He was stuck with them till the tour's bitter end.

"For the last week," he cut in, a smile of beautiful contentment on his face, "I kept saying to myself, 'If only those Callaghans look me up I won't be alone. I'll have at least one night when I can break away.' "

Now there were actually tears in his eyes. The poor man, this prison chaplain who had walked to the gallows with sixteen men, and whose only boast was that not one of these criminals entrusted to him had died in terror, and who, suffering from some fever that might be killing him, had been told to go to the Mediterranean and try and be happy, had in fact landed in a more depressing prison than the one he had left. You would have thought, looking at him now, that he had just jumped over the wall. My wife cut in to say he had asked immediately where they could buy something to drink and they had gone out together. Here they were now. Everything was fine. Then I noticed he was not wearing the priestly Roman collar. In France, he said, a clerical collar was taken as the mark of a Protestant minister. Therefore, an American priest had a choice between the soutane of the French priest, or the conventional white collar of the American businessman.

"Morley's been boxing," Loretto said. "Show him your shoulders. Oh, go on. Show him your shoulders," and then she explained to the priest, "If there are no marks on his face I know his shoulders will be all black and blue. Go on, Morley, don't be silly," and I had to take off my shirt. As usual, there were heavy welts on my shoulders. Shaking his head sadly, the big, rawboned, sandy-haired priest stood up. "If you were boxing with me those welts wouldn't be on your shoulders, they'd be on your jaw," he said. "I'd break you in two." "Would you now?" I said, thinking in his happiness he was going to lunge at me. "Ah, you're just a little guy," he said. But my wife had filled our glasses again.

It was twilight when we went out to eat. The priest, walking between us, his arms around us, chuckled to himself. At this hour his ladies would be wondering what he was doing, he said. But he had left a note for them; he had told them he knew a writer in Montparnasse, living among all the wild free artists, and the writer had a lovely wife, and he, himself, would be dining with them, spending the evening in the Latin Quarter. The note would put them in a terrible tizzy.

They would be sure he was off somewhere giving himself to the devil in the most dissolute company.

"What do you want to do?" we asked.

"Now, what would you be doing yourselves tonight?"

"Nothing. Just hanging around the Quarter."

"Could I just hang around with you, just be a part of your life tonight?"

Opposite the Dôme was the restaurant that had trays of hors d'oeuvres, more hors d'oeuvres than any restaurant in the neighborhood. Why shouldn't he have a chance to gorge himself? So we ate in this restaurant. Afterwards we moved down to the Coupole. On the street the girls loafed by. At nearby tables little groups argued; other patrons stared impassively at the other side of the street. But nobody was in a hurry. The whole bright corner under the Paris summer night sky must have suggested to the prison priest an oasis of warm, unhurried, careless conviviality. As he looked around he had an enchanted smile. Here at least no one would care what he did.

Since we rarely sat for long at the Coupole at that hour, we moved across the street to the Sélect where Titus joined us. A girl at loose ends, somebody's girl, sat down beside us waiting for her friend. Bob McAlmon came along. Then I remember someone saying, "Eugene Jolas and his wife are sitting over there at the Coupole. Are you going over?" and I half rose. Jolas was editor of *transition*, and had been printing stories of mine. Then I sank back in my chair, feeling a stab of resentment. Not many months ago, he had printed a piece by one of the aesthetes who had said that I was "immersed in life" and "ready for quick publication." It was not intended as a compliment, and looking at that Coupole deck of chairs, I said to myself jeeringly, What the hell am I supposed to be immersed in? Dreams? Like those French cutups, Breton, Aragon and Soupault? The naughty boys. And I worked myself up into such a state of combat I knew I had better not go across the street and speak to Jolas.

Then someone called me by name. My mouth fell open. A young newspaperman from my hometown, Toronto, was approaching us, all warmth and smiles. He was spending a weekend in Paris, he said, and heard I was in the Quarter. Innocently enough, I introduced him to the priest. "Father Tom," I said. "Yeah, a priest, eh?" said the Toronto news-paperman with an owlish leer. "Where's the Roman collar? Never mind. I get it." The leer was alien to the life of the Quarter. A cardinal, or Polly Adler, could have sat at any one of the cafés and no one I knew, meeting them, would have leered. And unfortunately the leer now was on the face of a man from back home. Home thoughts from abroad! The worst aspects of home. All that I liked about the Quarter, and all that I must have wanted to reject in my hometown, seemed to clash savagely. All the hostility I felt must have shown in my eyes as I explained that an American priest was not expected to wear the Roman collar in France; after all, he might be mistaken for a Protestant minister. The newspaperman quickly withdrew.

"Let him think what he wants," said the priest. "He's probably a very good-hearted fellow." And he was too. I had always liked him. But the leer—my hometown. Well, an odd thing happened a year later when I was back in Toronto. I had come to a party from a concert where I had had to wear a dinner jacket and black tie, and suddenly there was the newspaperman, whom I hadn't seen since the night at the Sélect, offering me an affable greeting. But he said, "Is that a real tie or one of those snappers?" Reaching out from the other side of the sofa which was between us, he gave the tie a little jerk to see if it would snap back into place. I was blind with rage. Leaping across the back of the sofa, I bowled him over, had him on the floor by the throat and was choking him. Afterwards I felt ridiculous. How could I explain I had suddenly remembered his alien leer that night in Paris?

"What's that pale yellow drink?" asked the priest. "I'll try one." We told him he should be careful of the Pernods. "Now don't be foolish," he said. "It's just a sweet drink and it tastes like licorice with water in it. No drink ever gave me any trouble." Well, we had warned him.

While he drank one Pernod and then another, we invited him to observe our little streetwalker, who was busy as always at that hour on the strip of pavement extending from the Sélect halfway over to the Gare Montparnasse. Every night we watched her plying her trade. A short stout girl, she was hardly beautiful, and incredible as it may sound, she usually wore a red dress. She worked out of a little hotel behind the Sélect. She had all the noble virtues of the Frenchwoman in real life, the woman at the market or at the cash register. She didn't loaf, there was no seductive silliness about her, nothing of the storybook dreamy siren with the Parisian flair. Just from watching her we could have given her a splendid character reference: honest, reliable, punctual, industrious. When she had picked up a customer, he would follow two paces behind her, both of them walking briskly, determinedly, as if she had found someone to help her clean up the kitchen, and they would vanish around the corner. A half hour later she would reappear, just as brisk, just as unsmiling, back on the beat. And regularly at 2 A.M. she would come from the hotel, always with a paper parcel under her arm, her head back, and hurry away home, as sensible and as domesticated a woman as you ever saw. I told the priest that after watching the girl night after night we had decided she had her place, a hard-won place, in the neighborhood pattern.

He made no comment. A strange smile on his face, he looked around the whole brightly lit neighborhood. Was he thinking of the hard monotony of the prison, comparing the prison life with this disordered idle sinful life flowing around him here? Could it be giving him some strange sense of peace? He could have been relating this abandoned café life to the prison life and his own fevers, making out of it all some satisfying total spiritual pattern. Or was it just the many Pernods he had insisted on drinking? But he did look happy and at peace. Around about two, we wandered happily along the boulevard. Music from the jazz band in the Jockey and crazy laughter floated out to the street. He wanted to go in. In that little smoke-filled room, where tipsy couples danced on a dime to wailing saxophones, he just watched. But as he watched he spoke about his convicts back home. Unfortunately, he also had another one of the sweet Pernods.

When we left the Jockey he didn't want to go back to the hotel. Holding our arms, he asked if he couldn't walk home with us. "I don't like to leave you," he said simply. So he walked us home and came in and he talked for an hour about his mother in Ireland, whom he would be seeing in a day or two, and for the last time, and how he would go back to the prison content.

At four, when he stood up, he lurched. He was surprised, hurt, unbelieving and terribly humiliated. We had warned him about the Pernods, and now he was bewildered. "Never in my life has this happened to me before," he kept muttering.

When we had driven him to his hotel, I remember that as we guided him into the lobby he turned. "Don't worry about me. I'll be up in the morning at eight."

"You can't get up at eight," I said.

"I have to," he muttered. "And I will. I told those women I had seen them for the last time. I told them they were malicious, uncharitable, backbiting and small-souled, and I was glad I would never see them again. And I won't. Don't worry. I'll catch that plane. I have to." Laughing a little, very moved, he put his arms around my wife and kissed her. He put his arms around me, too. "God bless you both," he whispered, steadying himself, and he walked slowly into the hotel.

It had been such an innocent evening, just sitting around. All he had done was drink too many Pernods, a drink he was unaccustomed to. Yet he left us feeling like Samaritans who had rescued a good man who had fallen among thieves. We had given him a good memory to take back to his penitentiary.

It was our weekend to have callers. We had another one. We had got up very late—it was actually early in the afternoon. Too lazy even to go out for something to eat, we nibbled at some croissants, and had some of the champagne. It was a clear warm sunlit day. Our Russian landlady, rouged and buxom, her hair freshly tinted, came and asked if we would like a drive around Paris. Well, the car was outside. It was a taxi. The swarthy and rather sinister-looking taxi driver was introduced to us as a colonel. A czarist colonel indeed he was, middle-aged now, who had fled from the Bolsheviks and was reduced to driving a taxi in Paris. He was obviously our Russian lady's lover. Since he had no English and even less French than I had, our madame kept him company in the front seat while we sat in the back. Rolling grandly around Paris through the Bois, and out to the country, he sat in utter silence. Out of politeness, Loretto and I didn't want to talk in English; they did not want to shut us out, talking in Russian. Yet we didn't get home till nearly seven.

Then on Sunday, in the middle of the afternoon, we had another caller. Loretto had washed out some handkerchiefs. While they were still wet she had smoothed them out flat on the windowpanes so the strong sunlight would dry and stiffen them. An hour later a knock came on the door. It was Scott Fitzgerald.

CHAPTER XXII

He looked beautifully tailored and clear-eyed. His eyes were not quite blue, but hazel or green-flecked. He came in with that smiling grace which was so natural to him and which I found so attractive. He had been thinking about us, he said, and he wondered if we wouldn't like to go over to the Ritz and have some drinks. Then his eye caught the handkerchiefs smoothed out on the windowpanes and drying quickly in the sunlight. Childlike in his curiosity, he approached the window, touched one of the handkerchiefs and turned to Loretto. "What is it? What are you doing with these handkerchiefs, Loretto?"

"Just this," she said. Tearing one of the stiffly dried handkerchiefs from the pane she calmly folded it, and it looked starched and neat. Since she had no facilities for ironing, she said, this was the method employed. And Scott, musing, was simply delighted. He had her take another handkerchief off a pane so he could fold it himself. Did women often do this? he asked. How simple and wonderful it was. Oh, he would certainly use it in a story. Day by day he sought out fresh little details like this one for use in his stories, he said. It was so difficult to come on something he hadn't used before. How pleased and charmed and grateful to Loretto he was.

In the little pause as we all smiled at each other, I waited uneasily for him to ask if I had spoken to Ernest about us all getting together. What could I say to him if he mentioned it? Tell him the truth? I couldn't bear to. Could I say, "The subject didn't come up, Scott"? What a look he would give me. The difficult moment passed easily. He was too sensitive a man to raise the subject bluntly. Raise it he would, of course, but in his own way when he had to. He had seen a copy of *The Great Gatsby* on the table and he picked it up, looking pleased. The sale of the book had been very disappointing to him, he said. Not that it hadn't done reasonably well, but no one would have called it a big seller. But there had been an explanation. "It was too short a book," he said. It was the one thing that was the matter with the book. "Remember this, Morley. Never write a book under sixty thousand words."

I had been getting ready to go out with him. When I had combed my hair and put on my coat I said, "Well, let's go."

But he was appraising me, consternation in his face. "Would you go over to the Ritz," he asked in a shocked tone, "wearing those sandals?"

They were the sandals I wore around the Quarter, as others, too, wore them. Smiling, I was about to tease him and ask what was the matter with sandals in the Ritz? But Loretto, who had seen the pain in Scott's eyes, said, "Im-

agine, Scott. Morley didn't notice he still had his sandals on."
And I said, "I'm excited. Wait, I'll put on my shoes." We
fell in with his attitude so willingly that the sudden stiffness
in him vanished. In his turn he had to explain himself.

Did I know Louis Bromfield? Well, Bromfield and his wife,
who lived in some style in a château outside Paris, had invited him and Zelda to dinner. When they arrived at the
Bromfield house they found Louis receiving them in his slippers. It was a mark of such disrespect it couldn't possibly be
overlooked; it showed what the Bromfields thought of the
Fitzgeralds. The Fitzgeralds had never visited the Bromfields
again.

Remembering Scott telling this story, I marvel at the little
things that shape the relationships of men; only the little
things seem to do it. Not great matters of principle, or ar-
ticles of faith, but fancied slights, a little detail acutely ob-
served that is supposed to reveal how things really stand
between friends. This matter of the slippers! Years later when
I met Louis Bromfield I told him this story about his slippers.
Wide-eyed, not smiling at all, full of wonder, he explained
that he always wore those slippers in his own house when his
guest was someone he felt close to. He had often wondered
why Scott had turned against him.

In my case I had got out of my sandals and into my shoes
in time. Scott seemed to be satisfied I had intended no disrespect to him or to the Ritz.

In the hotel, where he had the air of being at home, he
exuded some of that satisfaction he had shown when we had
been with him in the Joyce shrine, the Trianon. In deference
to Loretto we did not sit at the bar; we were at a table in the
corner, but I think he would have been more satisfied with
the rightness of things if we had been at the celebrated long

Ritz Bar. Again I waited for him to ask about Hemingway.

"Do you know, Morley," he said in that sweet quiet unspoiled tone, "you have written some of the finest stories in the English language." Taken aback, I tried to laugh. Those strangely colored eyes of his were on me, and if I clowned I knew I would be insulting him. His head on one side, he reflected, a wistful expression on his face. His extraordinary charm seemed to be in this unspoiled frankness; he could make you believe he was merely telling you something he had known for a long time. Obviously he had come out that afternoon with some hunger in him for talk, a gnawing necessity to express his interest in writing. How unlike Hemingway he was, I thought. You had to draw Hemingway out. And if Hemingway was working on a story, he was almost superstitious in his refusal to talk about it. He believed that if you talked about it before doing it, something was lost in the talking that should have gone into the writing. Now with Scott I was delighted to be my opinionated self.

Had I seen Gertrude Stein yet? he wanted to know. No, and I no longer had any curiosity about the grand lady. If Scott was interested in Miss Stein, he could have her. For my part, she had written one book, *Three Lives.* Having waded through *The Making of Americans,* and those stories of hers like "As a Wife as a Cow, A Love Story," I had done a little brooding over her. Abstract prose was nonsense. The shrewd lady had found a trick, just as the naughty Dadaists had once found a trick. The plain truth was, as I saw it, Gertrude Stein now had nothing whatever to say. But she was shrewd and intelligent enough to know it. As for her deluded coterie, well, I had no interest in finding one of them who would lead me shyly to her den.

My vehemence delighted Scott. Angular opinions also

came from him. He had taken some kind of a scunner to
André Gide. Perhaps it was because Gide was presiding over
the literature of France as I claimed Gertrude Stein was presiding over her little coterie. We agreed Gide was a second-
rate novelist. I put in a word for his intellectual curiosity.
We talked of Proust. Scott was dismayed by my refusal to go
on with Proust. I explained that Proust was the kind of a
great writer who got into your blood, and I knew he was not
right for mine.

Suddenly Scott began to talk about himself, making odd
candid remarks as if he would suddenly see himself against
the background of the people and events we were talking
about. Now he said most disarmingly, "Do you know what
my own story is? Well, I was always the poorest boy at a
rich man's school. Yes, it was that way at prep schools, and
at Princeton, too."

What was there to say to him? We had been talking only
about writing. Now he seemed to be trying to explain why
he felt driven to have such commercial success with his own
writing. "Do you know I'm a millionaire now?" he asked
simply.

Our little smiles didn't put him off. He argued sensibly
that any man who had an income of fifty thousand a year
was ranked as a millionaire. Wasn't it so? Our confusion
came from suspecting he didn't have a million dollars in capital. We were right. But we were overlooking the fact that a
writer's capital was the writer's talent. Since this thing he
had himself, which was his capital, brought him in fifty thousand a year, very well, then wasn't he to be ranked as a millionaire?

He was indeed, we agreed. But as he grew more confi-
dential he was more troubled, and he looked unhappy. He

had to write eight stories a year for the *Saturday Evening Post* at four thousand dollars a story. Oh, so I thought four thousand dollars a story was a lot of money, eh? Well, in view of the value of the storywriter to the big circulation magazine, he was actually being underpaid. Anyway, he, himself, had to be always looking around for material for those eight stories; he had to be working on them all the time, never resting, day by day picking up stuff like that bit about the handkerchiefs. Yet he also had to find time to turn to the work that was the core and hope of his whole life—his novel. At the present moment the novel—it was *Tender Is the Night*—was going very, very slowly. He couldn't get time. My God, there never was enough time. And when he found this time he couldn't seem to tap his imagination at will—not to his satisfaction.

I remember drawing back and looking in wonder at this slender, charming and secretly tormented man. This was the man who was supposed to be leading a crazy disorderly life. Yes, he did get a little drunk, did crazy things, and people thought of him as the wild, irresponsible playboy of the era. Yet what fantastic energies he had stored in him, what power of concentration while at the same time he watched over the wife whom Hemingway had called crazy! Here he was telling me of a production which could only come from an exacting rigid discipline. What haunted him, I was sure, was that he gave only his spare time to the work that was closest to his heart. Well, it was up to him. I became subdued. He made me feel lazy, as I was, and it seemed incredible that a man as knowing as Ernest could talk of him as if he were simply an alcoholic. He worked much harder than Ernest did. In fact he made me feel I didn't work at all. Drinking champagne cocktails, we talked on until after six. Then he told us he was supposed to take Mary Blair, the actress who had been Edmund Wilson's wife, to dinner. Could he meet us at one of the cafés afterward? We suggested the Lilas. We went out and got into a taxi.

When we were dropping him off he said suddenly, "Wait a minute." Pulling out his wallet, he counted his bills, and looked vague. "I may not have enough money," he said. "Have you got any money, Morley?" The two hundred francs, worth eight dollars at that time, which I had in my wallet I gave to my millionaire. To me eight dollars was eight dollars. I knew I wouldn't see it again, but I also knew that Scott, under similar circumstances, would have thrust eight dollars into my hand.

We were there at the Lilas, at our table under the chestnut tree, when Scott arrived with Mary Blair. She was a nice, shy woman who did not seem to know Scott intimately. Although he must have gone on drinking at dinner, it had only put him in a more lighthearted mood. Somewhere along the way—it may have been that he had gone home before meeting Mary Blair—he had acquired the most elegant felt hat I had seen in Paris; in color it was lighter than pearl-gray, almost white.

I remember that evening at the Lilas because the talk was idle, playful; anything said came out at random and mainly for laughs. For no reason, Scott said suddenly, "Do you know I predate Sinclair Lewis?"

"Well, you certainly don't look it," my wife said, thinking he was kidding. "You look young enough to be Lewis' nephew."

"I'm not kidding," he said. "I predate him as a writer. I had a success with *This Side of Paradise* before he had any success. I was an established writer before Lewis was. What do you think of that?"

"You poor old guy," I said.

Some musicians had appeared under our chestnut tree. They played their violins and I could look up and see the stars; and then we began to laugh, for the musicians were playing the American popular song "Ramona," and it made us feel nostalgic there under the trees. Scott, one elbow on the table, had been looking gravely at Loretto. "You know, Loretto," he said impulsively, "every time I look at you I see old castles behind you." This charming remark came from him as if it had been in the back of his mind for a long time; the charm of it was that you couldn't doubt that he meant it. The remark and the warm little scene made me feel again that he had some fixed place in my life, for I was suddenly reminded that in my college days at the dances, the last dance, the one I would have with Loretto, would be the song "It's Three O'clock in the Morning," which was the song he had often mentioned in his work.

Perhaps the musicians were making us think of home, or maybe it was the presence of Mary Blair, for Scott started talking about Edmund Wilson. He had reverence for Wilson, but now he was talking about an amusing evening and a little ditty of Wilson's. He had me say it with him, but all I remember now is, "Come on, pup, lift your paw up . . ."

When Mary Blair and Scott were leaving I said, "That's the grandest hat I've seen in Paris, Scott."

It was an Italian hat, he said. Taking it off, he gave it to me. "Take it, I want you to have it," and he put it on my head. I gave it back to him. A little more grimly, he put it back on my head. We kept exchanging the hat. The stubbornness I feared most in him began to show in his face. But my wife said firmly, "I simply won't have Morley take that lovely hat from you, Scott. Give it back to him, Morley." When he saw that he would have to struggle with her, too, he shrugged; he was defeated but content, and we parted for the night.

Next day two volumes of Proust were delivered to our place from Brentano's, with a note from Scott. I was to go on with Proust whether I wanted to or not.

When I saw Hemingway, I told him that Scott had talked for hours about writing and it had been a splendid, stimulating conversation. I had liked Scott's shrewd opinions, a quick fine intelligence, extraordinary perception and tireless interest, and I remember that Ernest merely shrugged, unimpressed. I didn't seem to be telling him anything new about our mutual friend. Unyielding, he said Scott found it necessary to talk a lot to writers like me who were doing what they wanted to do in their own way. Scott himself, doing those *Post* stories, felt driven to be with more experimental writers, he said. Since Scott couldn't get going with his own novel, it consoled him to show interest in the work of any writer he admired.

Ernest was simply unbudgeable. It was depressing. Was no one else to have an insight about Scott? Was Scott's story written and no line ever to be changed? A drunk who knew he was failing himself and his talent? Later, I found out that Ernest had even told Perkins he wanted to keep away from Scott. But I remember that as I talked to him that day, I felt his explanation that Scott as a drunk was a nuisance didn't tell the whole story. He seemed to have some other feeling about him, some other hidden resentment. I remembered, too, that in the beginning, five years ago, before he had met Scott, he hadn't expressed any admiration of his work. But his strange resentment, if it was there, and that day, calm and deliberate as he was, I nevertheless felt it in him, was to be kept secret—if possible—as far as Ernest was concerned.

CHAPTER XXIII

Scott had asked me what I had been working on, and I had told him I had taken away from Perkins some chapters of a novel. Very inferior stuff, I had decided. I didn't want to publish it. Scott had insisted I show these chapters to him. I was to call in late one particular evening. Loretto had come with me, but she wouldn't go into the Fitzgerald place. Scott might want to sit around drinking, and Zelda might want to stay up too, she said. I could tell Scott I had to meet her at the Deux Magots.

Zelda came to the door. As soon as I saw her I knew I shouldn't have been there. Pale, haggard, dark patches under her eyes, she stared at me vaguely, then tried to smile and failed. I can remember the way the overhead hall light glinted on her blond head. "Hello, Morley," she said reluctantly. I asked for Scott. Then she told me in a worried tone that she and Scott had had no sleep for twenty-four hours. Some trouble over the theft of Scott's wallet in a night club. Forget I had called, I said hastily. As she nodded gratefully and I went to go, I heard Scott's voice. "Who is it?" he called out loudly from the back of the apartment. "Who is it?" he yelled again, more insistently. Shaking my head, I would have fled. But she put out her hand, sighing wearily. No, I had better speak to him, she whispered. "It's Morley," she called. He answered firmly, "Tell him to come in."

It must have been a kitchen that we entered. It was impossible to look around. My eyes went straight to the table where Scott was stretched out naked except for his shorts; a French maid was rubbing his legs and kneading the muscles gently with practiced fingers. "Hello," he said, turning his head, but remaining prostrate. "Sit down," and he half groaned. I stared at him as Zelda did, standing beside me. She had a deep perplexed frown. Her obvious anguish made me hesitate to sit down. I thought Scott was drunk. "I'll just pick up that manuscript," I said soothingly. "I'll see you tomorrow, Scott." "No. I'll give it to you myself," he said. But he didn't move. Again he groaned wearily. Then I saw that he wasn't drunk; he was half numb with exhaustion. The nerves in his legs kept twitching. He told me what had happened.

Years later, I realized that I had walked in on the aftermath of the scene he wrote about in *Tender Is the Night*. Last night he had been in a night club, he said. His wallet had been stolen. He had accused a Negro, the wrong Negro, and the police had come; there had been a humiliating scene, then long hours of police interrogation as he tried to undo his false accusation yet prove his wallet had actually been stolen. The accused man and his friends had turned ugly.

Dawn had come. The questioning, the effort to make an adjustment, had gone on, and he had despaired of ever getting out of the humiliating dilemma. Just an hour ago he had got home, having had no sleep. He was so exhausted he could hardly move.

While he told the wretched story, the maid went on gently massaging his legs. Under that bright kitchen light his humiliation, his exhaustion with the aftermath of some drinking, made him look like a corpse. Zelda had remained silent; she kept staring down at him with that awful frown. I longed to get away. Giving him a little pat on the shoulder, I went to leave. He sat up suddenly. Already he felt better, he said. Where were his trousers? We would talk. He pulled on his trousers, dismissed the maid, whose helpless look at Zelda was her only comment. Then Scott took a little practice walk around the room, his body erect; he always walked with his head up; he had no intellectual stoop. Then he went calmly into his study, got my manuscript and came out, shaking his head hopelessly. But the helplessness, the anguish in his voice now only expressed the difficulty he felt explaining his dislike of my abandoned manuscript: It was slow. It didn't grip him. What was it about? Why had I written it? What could he say about it? The manuscript now only added to his distress. Starting to laugh, I reminded him I had no intention of publishing the book. Hadn't I taken it away from Scribner's? Nothing could please me more than to hear that he agreed I should throw it away. Taking the manuscript, smiling reassuringly at Zelda, I told him I was sorry I had to rush away, but Loretto was waiting for me.

"Where are you meeting Loretto?" he asked bluntly.

"I told her I'd only be in here a minute," I said. "I've been here half an hour as it is. So long, Scott."

"Where are you meeting her?"

"We were going to the Deux Magots. So long."

"I'm coming with you," he said.

But I was halfway along the hall. Following me, he grabbed my arm grimly. What was the matter with me? Why didn't we want him with us now he had told me he was feeling much better and wanted to talk? Zelda pleaded with him to go to bed. He pushed her away as I kept on going to the door. "Wait," he called, showing his disgust with us. When that stubborn expression came on his face, Zelda said wearily, "You'd better let him go with you. I'm going to bed."

If he had been drunk I might have been impatient with him. But he seemed to me to be simply shattered by the experience of the night before and by his own exhaustion, and it might have been true, as he said, that in his nervous condition he wouldn't have been able to sleep, since he couldn't relax. It could be that he needed some company. So I waited while he put his coat on. Yet so far from being himself was he that he didn't bother putting on a tie. Clamping that beautiful white hat on his head, he said, "Come on," and opened the door.

Outside, Loretto, worried from having waited so long, had kept herself half hidden in the shadow by the entrance. "Hello there," she said, ready to complain, but hesitating as she looked at Scott. I protested I hadn't wanted him to come out. In her presence he had quickly recovered some of his charm, and on the shadowed street, away from the light, he sounded like himself. Loretto couldn't see why I was concerned. "Just one drink and I'll go home," he said to me. Getting between us, he linked his arm in mine. For about fifty paces he held on to my arm affectionately, I didn't notice him suddenly withdrawing his arm. We walked on to St. Germain des Prés.

It was the wrong place for Scott to be going in his condition. St. Germain des Prés with its three cafés, Lipp's, The Flore, and the Deux Magots, is a focal point, the real Paris for illustrious intellectuals. Painters and actors from other capitals, and expensive women came to this neighborhood too. André Gide might be having dinner at the Deux Magots. Picasso had often passed on the street. The Deux Magots, while remaining a neighborhood café, was a center of international Paris life.

It was a warm night, not too hot, and the terrace of this old café was crowded. We had some difficulty getting a table. We had a drink. Scott's drink had a peculiar effect on him. In his nervous exhaustion he had thought the drink would cheer him up. Instead it seemed to numb him. Stiffening, he looked puzzled. Another drink might make him feel like himself, he said. My wife was watching him. She liked him, and I saw her eyes grow desolate. His face had turned ashen. He looked sick. People were gaping at him. We could see some Americans at a nearby table whispering. Suddenly it was as if he had been recognized; his name had been whispered along the terrace. Many other Americans were there. That year Paris was crawling with Americans wanting to see everything, and having the money to see it, not knowing that in a few months the stock market would crash and the year of Panic would begin. There at the café they could even see Scott Fitzgerald! He had become a legend in America. All that was reckless, prodigal and extravagant, all the women who were beautiful and damned and golden, were associated with his name. Now there he was, just as they had heard, an alcoholic.

Having ordered the second drink, he agreed that he shouldn't have another one. He insisted on paying for the saucers. But his movements had become painfully slow. As he took bills from his wallet, some fluttered to the ground, and I stooped and picked one up. A little later my wife picked one up. Our faces angry, we kept putting the bills in his hand while he sat there so pale and desperate, his shirt open, the elaborate white hat at too rakish an angle. The elegant Scott! When I saw a man at a nearby table whisper to his woman companion as they gaped, then smiled, I hated this man's face. I hated all the gaping vacuous faces around me. I wanted to kick over all the tables. Finally Scott stood up. Carrying himself with all the stiff remnants of his dignity, he walked away with us. Little was said on the way back to his place. In fact he seemed quite sober. I told him we would meet later the next afternoon, and as he rambled into his apartment I realized how fond I was of him.

That night at the Deux Magots, he had been in a false light. Apparently he had been making a public spectacle of himself; a living picture of all the belittling stories that were being told about him. No one could know he hadn't had any sleep for twenty-four hours. Yet he had managed to be seen in this light—the profligate abandoned sinner! How unlike Ernest he was, I thought. In those days Ernest would have never let himself be seen in this ridiculous light. For me, they were both extraordinarily attractive men. But men seem to have some secret built-in directional guide that governs their relationship with the other people; it has nothing to do with shrewdness, or cunning or conscious calculation.

In those days, whenever Scott did something ridiculous, he was caught red-handed. But worse, he suffered for things he didn't do; he had a knack of making himself always look worse than he was. And having a generous open nature, and great pride, he must have suffered. On the other hand, it was intolerable to Ernest to be in a bad light. Yet such was his nature, and his attractiveness, that he only needed to wait; in the course of time, no matter what he had done, he would manage to emerge in a good light. At the beginning of this story, back in Toronto, I mentioned that I had noticed that newspapermen had already begun to magnify everything he did, making it all into an attractive story. In the long run, his quality for moving others to make legends out of his life may have been as tragic a flaw as was Scott's instinct for courting humiliation from his inferiors.

On leaving him, feeling restless, depressed from knowing that commonplace people love watching a superior man making a spectacle of himself, we wandered up to the Coupole. McAlmon and the two boys, a Frenchman and the fabled artist model, the woman of so many lives in Montmartre and Montparnasse, Kiki, were there. She was still beautiful, but quite plump now, and there was something of the clown in her lovely face. In about an hour we all began to feel restless and mischievous. What could we do? Where could we go? It was after midnight, but someone suggested we should have a party in the Whidneys' elegant apartment. It was true that the Whidneys were not there with us and might, indeed, be sound asleep in their cozy home. Down the street we went, laughing and giggling, and on the stairs to the Whidneys' apartment house we began to make a lot of noise. Going up the stairs ahead of me was Kiki, and being the lovely clown she was, she began to go up the stairs on all fours. Whereupon I reached down, and threw her skirt up over her head. Undisturbed, she continued to go on up on all fours while I played a drumbeat with both hands on her plump behind.

When we rapped on the Whidney door they both answered in their dressing gowns, and although little Mrs. Whidney had her hair up in curlers, they invited us in for drinks with considerable aplomb. It put Scott out of my mind. Next time I saw him, in the afternoon, he was clear-eyed and smiling.

CHAPTER XXIV

Look at it in this way. Scott didn't like McAlmon. McAlmon no longer liked Hemingway. Hemingway had turned against Scott. I had turned up my nose at Ford. Hemingway liked Joyce. Joyce liked McAlmon. Yet these men, often so full of ill will for each other, nursing the little wounds to their vanities, could retire to the solitude of their own rooms and work long hours—sometimes ten hours—a day at the work they loved which gave them their real dignity. Hemingway had an expression I could never quite get used to. He would say of someone, "He doesn't know how to behave." The social criticism, the ethical position behind this simple statement, in fact all the implications behind it, used to mystify me. However, McAlmon certainly was one of those who "didn't know how to behave." Yet he too could suffer and struggle to protect himself against too painful an indignity.

Around the Quarter, indignities, bitter or comical, were shared so frequently they became little more than part of the daily gossip. With Scott at the Deux Magots I had shared a painful indignity. A few nights later with McAlmon, I shared one that was absurd.

After nine, when we were in our chairs at the Sélect, McAlmon came along the street looking for us. It wasn't McAlmon's style to come openly looking for anyone. He would rather have it appear that he had just happened to encounter you. And tonight we could see he was serious and preoccupied. When an hour had passed, he looked at his watch. "Let's go and sit in the Falstaff," he said casually. We demurred. More unlike himself than ever, he coaxed us. "No, you go ahead and we'll join you later," I said. But he wouldn't have it that way. We were his good friends. Who else was there to sit with? Just because he had told an acquaintance he would be in the Falstaff at ten, we wouldn't abandon him, would we? So we went with him to the Falstaff and sat at a corner table. As he talked his eyes would shift around the room. I thought he was looking for his friend. In a little while a big six-foot Swede came in with a little guy. They sat at the bar. After they had ordered drinks from Jimmy, they turned and stared at McAlmon. "There he is," McAlmon whispered. His manner had changed. His aloof expression, his indifferent tone, his whole manner of lordly disdain had gone. "Why doesn't he join us?" I asked.

"His name is Jorgenson," McAlmon went on whispering. "I had some trouble with him last night in the Dingo. He said he'd be in here at ten tonight to beat me up—if I came."

McAlmon's weak smile, as his eyes met mine, was half apologetic. A little chill touched my neck. Suddenly I was nervous. As my wife's eyes met mine I could see that she, too, knew what was expected of me. McAlmon might have been an inch taller than me, but he was light and thin, and no battler, and if big Jorgenson came over to the table and started slapping him around, I was supposed to defend him. I had been brought along as his bodyguard. It was news to me that McAlmon was aware of my boxing dates with Hemingway. On only one occasion, the one I have mentioned, had I talked about boxing. But our part of the Quarter was like a little village. Evidently hundreds of eyes had watched Ernest and me coming along the street, Ernest carrying the bag. Yet it was possible even that Jimmy, the bartender, had talked, which may have been why McAlmon had suggested to Jorgenson they meet in the Falstaff.

In a sense, McAlmon had been my first patron. He had been the one who had peddled my stories around. Outrageous as he was, I did like him. No matter what McAlmon did, or how angry I got at him, I liked him. And if Jorgenson should come over and punch him on the nose, what choice did I have? But I was not a man who liked testing his courage. I hated it. Whenever some occasion arose that was to be a test of my courage I became gloomy and very quiet, and if, out of deference to my pride, I knew I would have to go through with it, I became almost inert. I did whisper bitterly, "I suppose I'm to look after the big guy." When McAlmon didn't answer, I knew how he was suffering from the indignity of his position, so I added, "If they come over here you keep your eye on the little guy, eh?"

The tables weren't crowded. There would be some room to move around if I could get from behind the table, I told myself. I had to have room to move around. Nervous and gloomy though I was, I prepared the campaign. Then I saw that big Jorgenson at the bar was talking to Jimmy. And I seemed to hear the conversation, or rather what I hoped might be the conversation, as Jorgenson looked over at our table and turned to Jimmy. Jorgenson would be saying, "Who's the guy sitting with McAlmon?" and I prayed that Jimmy would say, "Him! He always comes in here with Hemingway after they've been boxing. And Hemingway always has a cut mouth." Why shouldn't Jimmy say this to Jorgenson? Hey, Jimmy, look over at me. I'll smile and wave to you, I thought.

I don't know what Jimmy talked about, but big Jorgenson, listening, would look over at our table and try to grin derisively. Watching him, I met his eyes with what I hoped was cold aristocratic disdain. Jorgenson and his friend went on whispering. Laughing and joking, they would both turn and stare at McAlmon. Ah, but the great thing was they didn't get off their stools. At our table there had been no further conversation at all. Finally Jorgenson and his little friend, both with a weary, bored, yet self-conscious air, said good night to Jimmy. They left without a single belligerent glance in our direction.

I sighed with relief. McAlmon, too, enjoyed a quiet relaxing moment. Then he became himself again. The old knowing, superior and contented little grin came on his face. It struck me that he was consoling himself in his humiliating position with the knowledge that he had known what would happen, had planned it beautifully, had outthought, outmaneuvered big Jorgenson. Anyway, there he was, safe and sound and lordly again, rejoicing in the absurdity of the situation. We had a drink. It's too bad big Jorgenson wasn't famous. He was a mystery story writer, I believe. If he had been famous, McAlmon could have told the story, told how he had outwitted him and made him behave like a puppet, and with the story, dragged him down. A good story, one that got close attention and was eagerly repeated, was one that made a distinguished friend look ridiculous.

We all gossiped, I suppose, and malice is more to be enjoyed than the celebration of virtue. McAlmon would even take a crack at his friend Joyce. "One good thing about you is you're not influenced by Joyce," he said to me. "Let Joyce have his Irish tenor prose." A man had to stand up under this general belittlement. The good ones did. It could be said that Ernest, taking the attitude he did to Scott, was belittling him. Of course he was. But Scott stood up under it. I mean as a person he stood up. I never heard him make a single derogatory remark about Ernest. There is a story that he had some kind of envy of Ernest's great writing skill. It can't be true. My two friends may not have been seeing each other, and one, Scott, might be feeling hurt and rejected, but the personal loyalty he seemed so desperately bent on offering to Ernest used to embarrass me.

CHAPTER XXV

There were afternoons when I would meet Scott for a drink, just the two of us. He no longer suggested we all get together with the Hemingways. Knowing now how stubborn he was, I still waited confidently for him to say, "I think I'll come along with you and Ernest. Tell me where to meet you." If either Ernest or Scott had by any single gesture indicated I was not wanted around, I would have fled and said, "To hell with them." But Scott seemed to believe that his own loyalty to Ernest and his admiration for him would have to bring them together. Yet Scott and I, by this time, always seemed to find other things to talk about. He was a delight to me. I could tell him about a story I was planning and he would seem to be absorbed in it. I liked, too, the way he tossed off irrelevant bits of information. People should feel free with each other, he would say. Did I know why Louis XIV established the code of manners? So his subjects, whether eating or meeting each other, would know how to behave; if they were all required to do the same thing on a given occasion, then they were free from the embarrassment of wondering what to do; thus, they enjoyed a kind of freedom and ease with each other. A splendid idea! How often this matter of a code of behavior seemed to come up around the Quarter. What was it? A disguised search for right action? Or the inevitable snobbery. As I have said, we were all dreadful snobs.

At other times Scott would startle me. "Tell me something," he would say. "Do you feel you're a great man?"

Thinking he was kidding me, I would laugh. "It's not worrying me, Scott."

"I'm serious."

"Is it so important?"

"I think it's very important," he insisted. "False modesty is not involved. A great writer, a great man must, I'm convinced, know himself he's a great man." And there at the café that afternoon he sounded so quiet and sensible and he looked so distinguished as he meditated, his eyes turned inward, I almost agreed with him. But all the way down the line I was really at odds with him. To be great without ever wondering if you were great, that was the thing, I said. To be original without ever trying to be original. But a man had to have some arrogance; it was his defensive weapon.

Those afternoons with Scott were all good sunlit afternoons. At first, some of his opinions would seem to me to be childish—like his theory about Hemingway needing a new woman for every big book. After pondering over one of these insights, I would see that he always had some basis for his judgment.

One day he asked, "How carefully do you read reviews?"

"I read the first five or six reviews very eagerly just to see how the book is going to be received," I said.

"But how carefully do you go over them?"

"Unless some rare bit of insight catches my eye I don't read them carefully," I admitted.

It had always seemed to me that writing was like painting; only a few people knew when a painting was really good. In a publishing house there might be one man. In all America how many critics were there who were capable of submitting themselves to the object—the thing written—and judging it for what it was? I grew more eloquent. I sounded vehement. What was the whole academic training? I asked. A discipline in seeing a thing in terms of something else. Always the comparison. The poem, the story, had to be fitted into the familiar scheme of things, or it didn't exist and the academic man was lost. A work had to be brushed off if the critic couldn't comfortably make it look like something familiar to him. It had always seemed to me that most reviewers were simply protectors of the known things.

But Scott was impatient. Of course I was right, but I was missing the point. Didn't I ever learn anything from the bad reviews?

"Never," I said, "unless I have some extraordinary respect for the reviewer."

Well, it wasn't like that with him, he said. He read all reviews carefully; no matter where they came from, or how bad they were, he read them carefully. No, it wasn't a waste of time. There was always the chance that some reviewer, even missing the point, might make one helpful remark.

As he sat there talking so sincerely I seemed to see him alone at night in his study. I looked at him in wonder, the author of *The Great Gatsby*, pouring over some dumb unsympathetic review, hoping for one little flash of insight that might touch his own imagination, make him aware of some flaw in his work, make him a better artist.

The afternoon which was to reshape my relationship with both my two friends, Ernest and Scott, was a little different right from the beginning from the other afternoons. My wife and I were meeting Scott at his place and we were to sit at the Deux Magots. Zelda was busy with her ballet lessons. I have a clear picture now of the three of us, Scott, Loretto and myself, coming from the direction of his place. Then we stopped, looking at the St. Sulpice Cathedral with its tower ~ising against the blue sky, and I muttered something about St. Sulpice art. It was a name for bad Catholic art. Though Loretto and I had passed this church again and again, we hadn't gone in. I made a joke about Scott living in the shadow of bad Catholic art. It amused him. Then he said that he liked living near the Cathedral; he liked the neighborhood; he was always aware he was in the shadow of the Cathedral.

Close to the entrance now, he asked if we knew that this church had columns larger in circumference than any in Paris. And my wife said, "Why don't we go in and look at them? Come on, Scott."

"No," he said, half irritably, he wouldn't go into the church. If we wanted to go in and walk around a column, he would gladly wait outside for us. "Oh, come on," my wife said, taking his arm. Firmly he detached his arm as he shook his head stubbornly. Since we were at the door of the church, going in with us wasn't much to ask of him, was it? A little thing like looking at the pillars. So we kidded and coaxed him. "I never go into the church," he said quietly. Suddenly his manner embarrassed us. We felt apologetic. "All right, Scott. But what's the matter?"

"I simply won't go into it," he said. "Don't ask me about it. It's personal. The Irish-Catholic background and all that. You go ahead."

So we left him standing in the sunlight while we went into the church. Rather quickly we paced around the circumference of one of the columns, then hurried out to Scott who was waiting, solemn and terribly unyielding. But his grim refusal to go in seemed to me to be a betrayal of some deep religious sentiment in him. We made some cheerful comment about the columns and went on our way.

As we were crossing the square he said quietly, "I was going to take your arm, Morley . . ."

"Well, so . . ."

"Remember the night I was in bad shape? I took your arm. Well, I dropped it. It was like holding on to a cold fish. You thought I was a fairy, didn't you?"

"You're crazy, Scott," I said. But I wished I had been more consoling, more demonstrative with him that night.

In the sunlight on the Deux Magots terrace we could see the old square-towered church of St. Germain des Prés. At night, when there was moonlight, the church was always a ghostly white. Was Descartes buried there? And to the right was the boulevard. The great houses there used to make me think of Balzac's duchesses, and the world of Proust. Then, without noticing how it happened, we found ourselves talking about Ernest. At first it was just an idle conversation. No one could have said that Scott was giving any sign of being under the power of a strange compulsion to be enjoying again the companionship of Ernest. He asked when I had last seen him and if we had been boxing. A few days ago, I said.

Then he began to reveal that no matter what might have happened between them, he still kept some wide-eyed loyalty to his own view of Ernest. Whether he was secretly hurt, feeling pushed aside and not needed, didn't matter. He began to tell me about all Ernest's exploits and his prowess and his courage. He told the stories as if he were making simple statements of fact. It seemed to give him pleasure to be able to tell stories about a man whose life was so utterly unlike his own. He gave Ernest's life that touch of glamour that he alone could give, and give better than any man. Ernest and the war. His wound. The time when Ernest thought he was dead. As he talked about bravery and courage, I grew impatient. These legends, this kind of talk, spoiled Ernest for me. I had as much affection for him as Scott had. I liked him for being the poet and storyteller he was, and I liked him for his warmth and availability to me, and the sweetness in him. I wanted to cut Scott off, but was afraid of offending him.

So I sat there, feeling that Scott was belittling himself. A lot of men had been close to death, a lot of men had been wounded, a lot of men had realized they were going to die. Why should Scott or anybody else make such a big thing of it? And as for courage, I didn't like all the talk about the loneliness of courage. It is outrageously untrue to pretend that the world is in a conspiracy to break a man's physical courage. Courage is the one virture that has had universal approval. I never knew anyone who was against it and wanted to see it broken. Even our worst enemies admire it in us, if we show it. Courage was life, and cowardice was death of the spirit, but it had always seemed to me the more you talked about courage the more you lost it and the more you began to fear cowardice. You feared yourself. And if you went around testing your courage, sooner or later you would drive yourself frantic and do some suicidal thing. A man who went around looking for challenges to his courage was right out of the phony days of chivalry, the days when men looked for fancied insults to an imaginary sense of honor. Cervantes in *Don Quixote* had destroyed forever all that nonsense. When I was with Ernest I never had these thoughts. I had them now, listening to Scott, who was making Ernest himself an unreal figure for me.

Then Scott began to repeat to me the story I had got from Max Perkins about Hemingway jumping into the ring and knocking out the middleweight champion of France. He told it as if he were letting me in on something, and he sounded a little awed. I could hardly conceal my exasperation with him. "Do you really think Ernest is that good?" I asked.

It didn't seem to occur to him that I might know better than he did. With a judicial air he pondered. "Ernest is probably not good enough to be the heavyweight champion," he said gravely. "But I would say that he is about as good as Young Stribling."

Young Stribling was a famous first-class light heavyweight fighter who was so good he was forced to fight heavyweights. "Look, Scott," I said to him, "Ernest is an amateur. I'm an amateur. All this talk is ridiculous. But we do have fun."

Not convinced at all, he shook his head. But then at last he said it; what he had been wanting to say for weeks. "Could I come along with you sometime?"

"Why don't you ask Ernest?"

"Is it all right with you? Do you think Ernest would object?"

Suddenly it seemed ridiculous to me that Scott, my friend, and Ernest's admirer, shouldn't be allowed to come with us some afternoon and be part of our common friendship. "Why don't you get hold of Ernest?" I said bluntly. "Get hold of him and say you were talking to me. Tell him point-blank you'd like to come along with us. Miró came with us. Why shouldn't you?"

CHAPTER XXVI

A week later, a little after three, I was at home doing some work on a new novel. My wife was puttering around. Later on I was to call for Ernest. A knock came on the door. And there were Scott and Ernest. The two old friends seemed to be in the best of humor. I could hardly conceal my pleasure. When I had come to Paris I had wanted to enjoy the company of these two men. Now they were together and they had come to my place—my friends. They had had lunch, Ernest said, and had decided to pick me up rather than wait for me. And Scott now was having his way. Ernest was carrying the bag that held the gloves. While I was getting ready, Scott talked to Loretto. But Ernest, having spotted a copy of *The New York Times* Book Review on top of our trunk, began to go through it carefully. I can still see him standing by the window, slowly turning the pages. I can see us waiting at the door until he had finished reading a review.

On the way to the American Club in the taxi, it seemed to me that Scott and Ernest were at ease with each other. There was no sense of strain and Scott looked alert and happy. We joked a bit. At the club—I remember the scene so vividly—I remember how Scott, there for the first time, looked around in surprise. The floor had no mat. Through the doorway opening into the next room, he could see two young fellows playing billiards. Scott sat down on the bench by the wall, while Ernest and I stripped. Then Ernest had him take out his watch and gave him his instructions. A round was to be three minutes, then a minute for a rest. As he took these instructions, listening carefully, Scott had none of Miró's air of high professionalism. He was too enchanted at being there with us. Moving off the bench, he squatted down, a little smile on his face. "Time," he called.

Our first round was like most of the rounds we had fought that summer, with me shuffling around, and Ernest, familiar with my style, leading and chasing after me. No longer did he rush in with his old brisk confidence. Now he kept an eye on my left and he was harder to hit. As I shuffled around I could hear the sound of clicking billiard balls from the adjoining room.

"Time," Scott called promptly. When we sat down beside him, he was rather quiet, meditative, and I could tell by the expression on his face that he was mystified. He must have come there with some kind of a picture of Ernest, the fighter, in his head. For Ernest and me it was just like any other day. We chatted and laughed. And it didn't seem to be important to us that Scott was there. He had made no comment that could bother us. He seemed to be content that he was there concentrating on the minute hand of his watch. "Time," he called.

Right at the beginning of that round Ernest got careless; he came in too fast, his left down, and he got smacked on the mouth. His lip began to bleed. It had often happened. It should have meant nothing to him. Hadn't he joked with Jimmy, the bartender, about always having me for a friend while I could make his lip bleed? Out of the corner of his eye he may have seen the shocked expression on Scott's face. Or the taste of blood in his mouth may have made him want to fight more savagely. He came lunging in, swinging more recklessly. As I circled around him, I kept jabbing at his bleeding mouth. I had to forget all about Scott, for Ernest had become rougher, his punching a little wilder than usual. His heavy punches, if they had landed, would have stunned me. I had to punch faster and harder myself to keep away from him. It bothered me that he was taking the punches on the face like a man telling himself he only needed to land one big punch himself.

Out of the corner of my eye, as I bobbed and weaved, I could see one of the young fellows who had been playing billiards come to the door and stand there, watching. He was in his shirt sleeves, but he was wearing a vest. He held his cue in his hand like a staff. I could see Scott on the bench. I was wondering why I was tiring, for I hadn't been hit solidly. Then Ernest, wiping the blood from his mouth with his glove, and probably made careless with exasperation and embarrassment from having Scott there, came leaping in at me. Stepping in, I beat him to the punch. The timing must have been just right. I caught him on the jaw; spinning around he went down, sprawled out on his back.

If Ernest and I had been there alone I would have laughed. I was sure of my boxing friendship with him; in a sense I was sure of him, too. Ridiculous things had happened in that room. Hadn't he spat in my face? And I felt no surprise seeing him flat on his back. Shaking his head a little to clear it, he rested a moment on his back. As he rose slowly, I expected him to curse, then laugh.

"Oh, my God!" Scott cried suddenly. When I looked at him, alarmed, he was shaking his head helplessly. "I let the round go four minutes," he said.

"Christ!" Ernest yelled. He got up. He was silent for a few seconds. Scott, staring at his watch, was mute and wondering. I wished I were miles away. "All right, Scott," Ernest said savagely, "If you want to see me getting the shit knocked out of me, just say so. Only don't say you made a mistake," and he stomped off to the shower room to wipe the blood from his mouth.

As I tried to grasp the meaning behind his fierce words I felt helpless with wonder, and nervous too; I seemed to be on the edge of some dark pit, and I could only stare blankly at Scott, who, as his eyes met mine, looked sick. Ernest had told me he had been avoiding Scott because Scott was a drunk and a nuisance and he didn't want to be bothered with him. It was plain now it wasn't the whole story. Lashing out with those bitter angry words, Ernest had practically shouted that he was aware Scott had some deep hidden animosity toward him. Shaken as I was, it flashed through my mind, Is the animosity in Scott, or is it really in Ernest? And why should it be in Ernest? Did Scott do something for him once? Is it that Scott helped him along and for months and months he's wanted to be free of him? Or does he think he knows something—knows Scott has to resent him? What is it? Not just that Scott's a drunk. I knew there was something else.

Then Scott came over to me, his face ashen, and he whispered, "Don't you see I got fascinated watching? I forgot all about the watch. My God, he thinks I did it on purpose. Why would I do it on purpose?"

"You wouldn't," I said, deeply moved, for he looked so stricken. For weeks he had been heaping his admiration of Ernest on me, his hero worship, and I knew of his eagerness for the companionship. Anyone who could say that he was under some secret and malevolent compulsion to let the round go on would have to say, too, that all men are twisted and no man knows what is in his heart. All I knew was that for weeks he had wanted to be here with us, and now that he was here it had brought him this.

"Look, Scott," I whispered. "If you did it on purpose you wouldn't have suddenly cried out that you had let the round go on. You didn't need to. You would have kept quiet. Ernest will see it himself." But Scott didn't answer. He looked as lonely and as desperate as he had looked that night when he had insisted on coming to the Deux Magots with Loretto and me. The anguish in his face was the anguish of a man who felt that everything he had stood for when he had been at his best, had been belittled.

"Come on, Scott," I whispered. "Ernest didn't mean it. It's a thing I might have said myself. A guy gets sore and blurts out the first crazy thing that comes into his head."

"No, you heard him. He believes I did it on purpose," he whispered bitterly. "What can I do, Morley?"

"Don't do anything," I whispered. "Forget the whole thing. He'll want to forget it himself. You'll see."

He moved away from me as Ernest returned from the shower room. With his face washed, Ernest looked much calmer. He had probably done a lot of thinking, too. Yet he offered no retraction. For my part, I tried to ignore the whole incident. Since we had had a good two or three minutes' rest to make up for the long round, why couldn't we go on now? I asked. It gave us something to do. Ernest and I squared off.

Scott, appearing alert and efficient, and hiding his terrible sense of insult and bitterness, called "Time." As I look back now I wonder why it didn't occur to me, as we began the round, that Ernest might try to kill me. But between us there was no hostility. The fact that I had been popping him, and then had clipped him and knocked him down, was part of our boxing. We went a good brisk round, both keeping out of trouble. When we clinched, my eye would wander to Scott, sitting there so white-faced. Poor Scott. Then suddenly he made it worse. The corner of a wrestling mat stuck out from under the parallel bars, and when I half tripped on it and went down on one knee, Scott, to mollify Ernest, called out foolishly, but eagerly, "One knockdown to Ernest, one to Morley," and if I had been Ernest, I think I would have snarled at him, no matter how good his intentions were.

But it was to continue to be a terrible and ridiculous afternoon for Ernest. It is a wonder he didn't go a little mad.

As soon as we had finished the round, that slender young fellow who had been playing billiards, the one wearing the vest, who had been standing watching, his cue in his hand, came over to us. He might have been an inch taller than me, but he was very slender; he couldn't have weighed more than a hundred and thirty-five pounds. A student probably. "Excuse me," he said to Ernest in an English accent. "I've been watching. Do you mind me saying something? Well, in boxing it isn't enough to be aggressive and always punching. If you don't mind me saying so, the real science of boxing is in defense, in not getting hit."

It was incredible. The student was prepared to tell Ernest how to box. I was shocked and fearful. Both Scott and I, gaping at the student, must have been sharing the same sense of dread. What would Ernest do? A man can stand only so many mortifications in a single afternoon. If Ernest had grabbed the presumptuous fellow's billiard cue and broken it over his head, I wouldn't have been surprised.

Yet Ernest, after waiting a moment, the moment of astonishment, asked quietly, "Do you think you could show me?"

"Well, I could try," the young fellow said modestly.

"Good," said Ernest. "No, wait. Don't show me. Show him," and he pointed at me. "I'll watch."

Now I, in my turn, felt a twinge of resentment against Ernest. The student didn't want to show me how to box; he wanted to show Ernest, didn't he? I was to be used as a tuning fork. And who could tell whether or not this slender fellow was an English lightweight champion? Scott hadn't said a word. Nor did he speak as he removed Ernest's gloves and laced them on the intruder. Squaring off with him, I was ready to cover up like a turtle. As we circled around each other, I tried warily to make him lead at me. A feeble left did come at me, but it seemed to be only a feint. This boy was obviously a counterpuncher. Sooner or later I would have to lead at him. He had probably worked with pros. He was probably a hooker; I had always been rattled by a good hooker. I would lead now, then he would blow my head off. But gradually I was forcing him into a corner. Suddenly I caught a familiar expression in his eyes. I could see he was more scared of me than I was of him. As I began to flail away happily at the young fellow's head, Ernest suddenly shouted, "Stop!"

Now Ernest had a very good moment. In a beautiful bit of acting, not a trace of mockery in his tone, he said to the student, "I think I understand what you meant. Now show me." Ernest now unlaced my gloves. I in turn laced them on him. The student looked pale and worried. Against me he had been inept and he knew it, and he knew, too, that he had in effect invited Ernest to knock his block off. Then he caught the derision in Ernest's eyes. Shaking his head apologetically, he would have withdrawn. "No, come on. You've got to show me," Ernest insisted.

The student still believed, no doubt, that Ernest was wide open. As he faced him he crouched a little, his hands high, ready to demonstrate his defense. Smiling faintly, Ernest spread his legs, stood rooted there like a great stiff tree trunk, and simply stuck his long left arm straight out like a pole and put his right glove on his hip, contemptuously. He refused to move. It was a splendid dramatic gesture of complete disdain. In fairness to him, he didn't try to clobber the boy, didn't try to strike a single blow. As the student circled around him, he, himself, turned slowly like a gate, the hand still on his hip, the great pole of an arm thrust out stiffly.

The student grew humiliated. Without hitting a blow or being hit, he quit. "I'm sorry," he said. "I really haven't done much boxing. I've read a lot about it. It looked much easier than it is," and he held out his gloves to me and let me unlace them. I didn't feel sorry for him. He went back quickly to his billiard table.

The student's absurd intervention, adding to the general sense of humiliation, must have put Scott more on edge. He must have felt bewildered. Yet now my two friends began to behave splendidly. Not a word was said about the student. We were all suddenly polite, agreeable, friendly and talkative. I knew how Scott felt; he had told me. He felt bitter, insulted, disillusioned in the sense that he had been made aware of an antagonism in Ernest. Only one thing could have saved him for Ernest. An apology. A restoration of respect, a lifting of the accusation. But Ernest had no intention of apologizing. He obviously saw no reason why he should. So we all behaved splendidly. We struck up a graceful camaraderie. Ernest was jovial with Scott. We were all jovial. We went out and walked up to the Falstaff. And no one watching us sitting at the bar could have imagined that Scott's pride had been shattered.

Yet he had some class, some real style there at the bar. I told Ernest that Scott agreed with me that the chapters of a novel I had started ought to be abandoned. I remember Ernest saying, "There are two ways of looking at it. You can think of a career, and would it help your career to have it published? Or you can say to hell with a career and publish it anyway." Scott said he was glad I wasn't going on with the book. As we exchanged opinions I noticed that two of the patrons, two young fellows at a nearby table, were craning their necks, listening and watching. And I laughed and said that by tomorrow word would go around the café that I, shamefully, was letting Fitzgerald and Hemingway tell me what to do about a book. Ernest said, "What do you care? We're professionals. We only care whether the thing is as good as it should be." And again, as I say, anyone watching would have believed that we were three writers talking about a literary problem. No one could have imagined anything had happened that could be heartbreaking. Well, I had come a long way to have my two friends get together with me, and here they were.

CHAPTER XXVII

My two friends, when I saw them separately, seemed to be wonderfully untroubled about each other. Ernest would have had me believe he hadn't given a second thought to his words to Scott in the American Club. Nothing worth mentioning again had happened. When I saw Scott, he was superb too—he didn't even ask for Ernest. And I joined in the general pretending. I became a man who "knew how to behave" as Ernest would say. I managed to give the impression of being completely unaware of any deep disappointments and hidden resentments. How could bitterness flare up if they weren't seeing each other? I asked myself. For now that July had come they were both to go away, Ernest south, probably to Spain, and Scott would soon be off to the Riviera. What could be better than to have everybody go away for awhile? Everybody off to the seashore! I was glad they were going.

While they were away I could relax a little myself and pretend that we would all be the best of friends when they returned. I knew I ought to have stopped pretending. But pretending is contagious. It makes life more agreeable.

I should have said, "Ernest, I think you've got Scott all wrong." But Ernest was a strange ingrown man who could make you feel his resentments were born of some deep primitive wisdom. Besides, I didn't want to keep reminding him I had had a hand in his embarrassment. If I kept prodding him about Scott, if I dared to suggest he might owe Scott an apology, I was afraid his vivid imagination would start working on me, and he wouldn't want to see me either. Let the whole thing blow over, I thought.

July was a hot month. In the strong afternoon sunlight the Dôme, the Coupole and the Sélect, the whole corner, had a bright hard look. But too many summer soldiers had come to town. Visitors dropping off buses sat around for an evening, then disappeared. At night now Loretto and I would wander off with someone to other neighborhoods. There were the *bals musettes* down by the Bastille, the Pigalle bars, and the Hôtel du Caveau on the rue de la Huchette; then back to our roosting place to find amusement in the antics of strangers. In the hot weather we had a nightly supply of comics. An Englishman and his wife would be giving a remarkable performance, discussing *Lady Chatterley's Lover*. Talking quite rationally at first, the lady would suddenly say, "But those forget-me-nots. Why, that woman put a wreath of forget-me-nots on that man's . . . well, an unmentionable part of his body." And her husband, his face suddenly bursting red with outrage, "It's incredible," and turning on us, his voice quivering, "Are you prepared to say those forget-me-nots on the man's privates isn't rubbish?" As a man and wife they suddenly had a perfect union in their sense of outrage. And we knew they themselves didn't go monkeying around with forget-me-nots.

Other faces, other voices had become familiar. The voices of the two young Jews who had become Catholics would drift over to us, one saying softly to the other, "Notre Baudelaire," the other nodding in his enchantment; or from the two boys having their week in town, two who loved Jane Austen, would come the adoring words, "Dear Jane . . ."

But all that month I didn't hear any arguments about economics or politics. No one stood up and shouted about the necessity of a social conscience. I remember that Hemingway had talked about Mussolini, and the Social Democrats in Germany, but he would talk as a shrewd observer; a man who had the political facts right out of the horse's mouth; he would be letting you in on what was going on. Yet there was no distinction in being against Fascism—everyone was. The Left—the Marxist? To me at that time it would have seemed incredible that writers within a few years would go running to commissars seeking direction. If I talked about Dos Passos, it was because I was interested in what he was trying to do with his material—society; he was against the social fraud, the bourgeois values. But who wasn't? At the cafés the writers and hangers-on—my God, now they seem to have been nearly all hangers-on—were more interested in the revolution of the word than the world. Yet within a few months the stock market in New York was to crash, the depression was to begin, and the clients of those cafés who got money, no matter how little, from home, were to vanish one by one.

In those hot days when everyone else was going away, moving on, we had to make a move too. One morning after waking up, my wife showed me a little blood mark on her leg. What was it? It worried us. Next morning she had fresh little pinpricks of blood on her ankles. Alarmed, we wondered if she was suffering from some strange malady. Next night, in the very middle of the night, she suddenly threw off the covers and turned on the lights. A bedbug! We had never seen one. In the morning we summoned our Russian landlady and showed her the dead bug in the newspaper. "Ah, *pounais!*" she cried. Writhing with mortification, she explained that the grocery store below us had been fumigated. No doubt the bedbugs were driven up to her establishment. When we told her we would have to leave her, she understood. Her proud aristocratic Russian blood seemed to help her to understand. Her shame, mixed up with rage against the grocer, made us want to root for her. But nevertheless we moved to a little hotel on Raspail, and it was during that week that Scott told me that he and Zelda were going south to Nice.

The morning I met him at the Deux Magots, I remember that we talked quietly about our plans and about his hope of getting time enough to finish the novel. It still wasn't going right for him. Now I remember that the conversation stuck in my mind, and when *Tender Is the Night* finally came out, I felt Scott never did get Dick Diver, his central character, in focus.

There at the café he didn't ask for Hemingway. Maybe Ernest was in our minds, for Scott that morning seemed to have a stiff dignity. He had been treated without respect in my presence, and he had taken it; a little thing like that could make him want to avoid me, I knew. We assumed that I would be in Paris when he returned. As we walked away from the café, talking easily, I suddenly felt great affection for him. He hoped I would quickly finish the book I was working on. I remember he said, "Try and get something from a child's point of view as a contrast. It opens up another world. It lightens all the material." Then it was time for us to part. Suddenly he pulled his wallet out of his pocket, took out the bills, thrust the wallet at me. "Here, Morley, keep this wallet. I'd like you to have something of mine." And I said, "All right. Write your name in it then." Neither one of us had a pen. He put the wallet against a lamppost, and taking out his knife he scratched his name on the leather. We shook hands and he was gone.

Hemingway, too, had left town. So had McAlmon. In August all the people one knew had gone to a watering place or into the mountains or south to a seashore. Titus too had gone to Nice with Helena Rubenstein. Before he left he asked us to move to his handsome apartment just around the corner from the Dôme. He was a book collector. He had one of the finest book collections in Europe. While he was away he liked to console himself with the thought that he had someone in his quarters who was reading the books, not stealing them. Late at night I would sit up reading the later novels of Henry James. That style of his in those later books! I began to hate it. Not layers of extra subtleness—just evasion from the task of knowing exactly what to say. Always the fancied fastidiousness of sensibility. Bright and sharp as he had been in the earlier books, the fact was that James had got vulgar—like a woman who was always calling attention to her fastidiousness.

When Titus returned, Loretto and I began to believe that we were the last of the immovable figures around the Quarter. One night our friend Whidney, from the Chicago suburb, talked about the Basque country. Suddenly we wanted to go there. We went with Whidney. We stayed in Bayonne, where we became honorary members of the Bayonne Tennis Club. In the mornings we would play tennis and in the evenings go to the Casino in Biarritz, and I remember that one night on the way home we wandered into an elegant house without noticing it had a red light over the door. A woman, surely the world's most tolerant and cultivated madame, explained that my wife could not enter the room where her girls were, but if we would like it, two of her girls would come into our room and make a tableau for us. We had a drink and some sympathetic conversation with the madame, then my wife led the way out.

One weekend we crossed the border to San Sebastián and saw the bullfights. And then—well what could we see now that we hadn't seen before, what could we do we hadn't done before? That was the quest. There was Lourdes in the mountains. Lourdes and the miracles! So we took the train through the Pyrenees to Lourdes on the day of the Belgian National Pilgrimage to the shrine. The great mountain valleys were filled with mists and shadows, and mists lay on the peaks of the mountains. It was the kind of heavy lonely landscape that made me want to believe in angels as well as earthly creatures. It looked like a place of mysterious grandeur where men could trust their own visions. Peer Gynt could have come here, I thought, seeking something new that might finally satisfy him. And had I, too, just begun my own wandering from home?

Now I think that all of us in Montparnasse, McAlmon, Fitzgerald, Hemingway, Titus and even that Pernod poet were Peer Gynts who knew in our hearts we would soon have to go home. No, not Ernest. Could he ever really go home? Or for him, committed as he was to the romantic enlargement of himself, did there have to be one adventure after another, until finally there was no home? And what could be left for Scott when the glamorous wandering was over? When "a primrose by a river's brim, a yellow primrose was to him, and it was nothing more." My old theme. Nothing more; the wonder of the thing in itself. Right for me. But not for Scott.

I turned out to be a bad pilgrim, or perhaps I was still a dissatisfied Peer Gynt. I seemed to be able to notice nothing but vendors selling cakes and religious medals. And I muttered so often that I might as well be at a fair ground, I'm sure I spoiled things for Loretto. In the grotto we saw all the weathered crutches. We were in the great square when it was time for the sick and the crippled to be wheeled there to wait for the terrible moment when the priest would hold aloft the Blessed Sacrament. The square, set down in the mountains, was jammed with the faithful and the sick in chairs, who gazed raptly at the Blessed Sacrament which was being carried by the priest in a slow procession. As he moved past those in wheel chairs in the front row, the sunlight glinted on the golden chalice containing the Host. The sun's rays coming over the mountain peaks flooded the whole square in the valley. Finally the little procession turned back to the altar. Then there was utter silence. I had never before felt such a general tension within a silence. It was the moment of desperate prayer for the sick who were there waiting, the wild leap of faith.

Then I heard a cry, a moan. A cripple rose slowly out of a wheel chair, rapt, his face shining, and went staggering forward. He fell flat on his face. He sobbed. It was a terrible sound. In a chair beside me was a beautiful fair American girl who was trying to lift herself from her chair. Finally her head fell back, her eyes closed, and she wept but made no sound as the tears ran down her cheeks. All around us now was excited chatter broken with wild cries: *"Un miracle, un miracle."* Wheeling, turning, groping, shoving, they were all trying to get close to a miracle. Groups formed around those who claimed to have been touched by healing light. And groups were around the comics, too, who basked in attention. A middle-aged woman who kept tapping her shoulder explained that the arm had been hopelessly crippled. She held it out proudly. But the wise Frenchmen around her were smirking behind her back. They understood that she had grabbed the center of the stage.

The whole crowd had been broken into these little groups, and in each group was someone insisting his prayers had been answered. Those in the chairs were being wheeled back to the hospital where doctors would examine them. As I watched their faces I thought of the fair American girl and how the tears streamed down her face. My little prayer that afternoon was that her tears might have been from hope and not despair, and that in her hospital bed that night she would still have hope, still have faith that she would be cured, still be dreaming of going home. As we wandered away from the square, darkness came quickly from the mountains. Soon the night and the hills were all one and we were on our way back to Bayonne. Two days later we were back in Montparnasse.

Having finished my novel and with the September days passing slowly, I noticed we were always looking around restlessly for something new to do. I missed the excitement, the pleasure and surprise I had got out of the company of Ernest and Scott. I would have been glad to see McAlmon coming along the street ready to create a difficult situation, or bringing some news of Joyce.

In the tennis games at Bayonne, Whidney, who had taken lessons from a good pro, had always beaten me, but he had hated himself for finding it so difficult. My form was bad and he had contempt for the way I could get the ball back over the net, and even greater contempt for himself for not being able to blast me off the court. He maintained I was so bad I was good. One night at the café I looked at Michael Arlen and knew beyond all doubt he would have taken tennis lessons from the best of pros. How was his tennis form? I asked. It was great, he assured me. Whereupon I bet Whidney money Arlen could beat him in a match. We were all to meet at the Coupole next day and go off to the tennis court.

Next morning my wife, having looked at my flannels, said they were soiled. We agreed that Arlen, who was so dapper himself, and from whom we expected great style in tennis, would be insulted if his partner did not show up in immaculate flannels. I took them down to a corner laundry. The laundress promised to have them cleaned and ironed in two hours. At the hour when I was supposed to be meeting Arlen, I was sitting in the laundry watching the laundress trying to iron my pants dry. Arlen and Whidney were kept waiting an hour and a half. After my silly apologies we all went to the tanbark court. Arlen did put on a very stylish performance against Whidney. But of course, Whidney beat him easily. With superb aplomb Arlen stood before me, his backer and sponsor, and as if he were holding a club he flicked his wrists. "I have been playing too much golf," he explained. "It is a different motion of the wrists," and he walked away grandly.

With the nights getting a little cooler I would notice, sitting at the café, that I seemed to be waiting for something. Gradually I began to figure out what was troubling me. We seemed to have come to a resting place in Montparnasse.

Talking to Ernest I had said, "The Americans around here can't be Frenchmen, no matter how well they speak the language. If we are going to stay here it means really we have to become Frenchmen." And he had said, shrugging, "Who would want to stay?" Looking at him, I had gathered he had no intention of settling down in France. But then where would he go next? It had been my absolute conviction that he would never return to America and write about his own people in their cities and towns as he had done once in his little Michigan stories.

At the Sélect one night with Loretto, I remembered this conversation. I told her that if I were to stay on in France I should now be soaking up French culture. I should want to be with French writers. If I didn't want the French culture, then I was there in exile. Could the dream I had had for years of being in Paris been only a necessary fantasy? A place to fly to, a place that could give me some satisfactory view of myself? And she asked if Scott and Ernest too were in flight, and I said, yes, they were. Ernest would never again write about his own country. And Scott, as long as possible, would go on drinking and rushing to the Riviera.

"It's a kind of otherworldliness," I said, laughing, yet meaning it. And indeed it was my conviction now that for most men there had to be some kind of another more satisfactory world. (The primrose had to be anything but a primrose.) The saints, tormented by the anguish of the flesh, wanted to reject the human condition, the world they lived in. But whether saints or café friends there in Paris, weren't they all involved in a flight from the pain of life—a pain they would feel more acutely at home? It struck me then too that the French literature we had so much admired from Mallarmé to the surrealists was simply a rejection of this world and the stuff of daily life. The French writers stayed at home and exiled themselves in their own dreams. Then what would my own fantasy be? Loretto asked, lightheartedly. And rather grandly, to mask my doubt and wonder, I said I might have to forge my own vision in secret spiritual isolation in my native city. Joyce in exile had gone deeply, too deeply, into himself. But what if he had stayed in Dublin?

A week later, looking around the café, Loretto said idly, "Paris is lovely. We've been so happy here. But doesn't it strike you that this neighborhood is now like a small town for us?"

"Yes, the same faces always in the same places. And all the gossip. What do you say if we go to London?"

"Don't you want to see Ernest or Scott?"

"I've been thinking about it," I said slowly. "How do I know Ernest wants to see me?" I didn't tell her I had a hunch Ernest was back in Paris. I had been nursing a suspicion that Ernest, brooding over the indignities he had endured in the last encounter with me and Scott, had decided it would be better to avoid me. Why be in the company of someone who could only remind him of embarrassing moments? If I had revealed this suspicion to Loretto she would have said to me, "If you think he's back in town, for heaven's sake, why don't you look him up?" My egotism wouldn't let me go looking for him again. I had told myself I would leave it to him. If he were back in town and wanted to see me, he knew where to find me.

We booked our passage to London. In three days we were to leave the Quarter.

That night at ten we had come along Montparnasse from the rue de la Santé. The October nights had got much cooler and a heavy dampness seemed to be in the air, and even at that hour we saw derelicts huddling near restaurant doors. Later, when the chairs were piled on the tables on some of the terraces, these derelicts would sleep in the corner by the wall. We went to the Falstaff where we sat by ourselves. Often now we did not need any company. When we had been there only fifteen minutes Loretto said, "Good heavens, there's Ernest." He was at the door, looking around rather shyly or self-consciously. Big and dark he loomed up there in the doorway. Waving to him, I stood up, and I remember how he grinned coming toward us. His pleased warm friendly grin made me feel ashamed of my secret thoughts about this man who had meant so much to me. As he sat down he looked at my wife, shook his head and laughed, for she had had her hair cut short like a boy's. Titus and McAlmon had persuaded her that a short haircut would accentuate her handsome profile. When she asked Ernest why he was laughing, he assured her he liked her haircut very much.

We talked like old good friends. We told him we were leaving town. Never had he been more sympathetic and charming. He asked us if we were leaving France without seeing the Cathedral of Chartres. We were? How foolish. But we had only two days more. Then take a day and go to Chartres, he said. It was incredible that we would depart without making this pilgrimage. When we demurred, finding obstacles, he told us that he, himself, would drive us to Chartres in the morning. All we had to do was get up early and be at his house at eight thirty.

After he had left us I told Loretto how moved I had been to see Ernest come walking toward us. Our last trip anywhere in France should be with him, I said. And, of course, he was right. To have left France without seeing Chartres would have been criminal.

In the morning at the appointed hour we were at Hemingway's place. Not in months had I been up at such an hour. Half asleep as I was, it was hard for me to be immediately charming and available. I went in to get Ernest. I remember that his sister, a tall dark girl, was there. As we came down the stairs, he stopped halfway down and asked how we would like to go to Longchamps? He had been given a hot tip on a horse, a really hot tip. Of course it was up to us, since he had offered to drive us to Chartres and had told us how important it was to see the Cathedral, but what did we think about us all going to the races? His boyish eagerness was usually irresistible, but now I looked at him blankly. "We'll ask Loretto," I said. Just last night he had convinced me that I was guilty of criminal negligence in not going to Chartres. Outside he said hopefully, "You'd like to go to the races, wouldn't you, Loretto?"

But she had seen the expression on my face. "Whatever Morley wants to do," she said hesitantly. "I think you convinced us last night we ought to see Chartres."

But the races, if we could all go to the races, and he had thought—well— In the presence of our embarrassed silence he yielded. Leaving us he went back upstairs and spoke to his wife. My own wife whispered to me it was plain he was exasperated. Perhaps we had better go to the races. No, I said stubbornly. Who's idea was it to go to Chartres? Then he came out and we got into his Ford.

With the three of us in the front seat the little struggle between Ernest and me seemed to have ended. Driving out into the country he didn't mention the races again. He seemed to be splendidly himself. We talked and laughed.

We were in such good humor I asked suddenly if he had heard from Scott. He hadn't heard from him at all, he said. Trying to draw him out I went on talking about Scott, hoping he would show some awareness of Scott's hurt feelings. He seemed to have forgotten the whole incident. Nothing about Scott was bothering him.

As we drove along I watched his face. It was incredible that he could be unaware that he had shattered our friend. Speeding on the highway, I tried to get him to say what he thought about Scott's writing. I was no more successful than I had been five years ago in Toronto. I think now he rejected Scott's whole view of the world.

And yet this strange warm beguiling man, who was there on the seat with Loretto between us, could have had another need, a need to believe that as an artist he had never been dependent on the help of anyone else. We had started talking with enjoyable malice about friends. We made some jokes about Ford. As I said before, his respect for Ford had gone. Yet Ford in the beginning had written that Ernest was "the best writer in America." Then he explained McAlmon's crazy life. The trouble with McAlmon was that he had had a brother, or a cousin, who had been an idolized football player, and McAlmon had been no good at games. Yet McAlmon, Ernest's first publisher, had really helped him along the way. And Sherwood Anderson in the beginning had praised Ernest to the skies. And Scott! Hadn't he gone to Scribner's about Ernest's work? For one reason or another Ernest had rejected all these old friends. Warm, likable and lovable as Ernest was, did he have some secret need to protect his ego from anyone who might have a minor claim on him?

Then he became very talkative about writing. He talked

about style, and we were in happy splendid agreement. The decorative style, the baroque based on a literary adornment of perceptions, was an affectation in our time, he said. Only the clear direct stripped statement belonged to our time, and it wasn't just a matter of what you could or couldn't do. And another thing. If it came down to a question of scholarship about these matters, no one he knew had a more scholarly awareness of what was involved than John Dos Passos, and Dos agreed with him, he said.

And he had a little trick of conversation that amused and delighted me. He would say writers caught on because of their affectations, their tricks of style, a point of view; then would add, "But we know. . . ." That "we" became fascinating. There were real writers, the "we"; the others were nothing in themselves. But we had come to Versailles. He was sure we would want to see the grounds and the Palace.

When we were in the great Hall of Mirrors I noticed that Ernest, walking with Loretto, seemed to be in no hurry to have us get on our way. He would let me wander away, bemused by the seventeenth-century love of perfect balance and form. Sometimes I would return for a few words, then go off by myself again. Finally Ernest looked at his watch as I joined them. "Loretto," he said hopefully, "if we leave now we'll have time to get back to Paris and see the races. What do you think yourself?" Her expression told me she was weakening. If she had only nodded her head to him the thing would have been settled. But then I realized that he had counted on the long stopover at Versailles satisfying us and again it was as if we were boxing. Now he had feinted me out of position. Loretto would be agreeing, too, that he had been generous enough to come this far. I'm not going to turn back now from Chartres, I thought grimly. Not just to see a horse race. My wife said, "Well, what do we do?" and I said, "I'll regret it all my life if I don't see Chartres. Come on, let's go."

As we got into the car I knew that in Ernest's place I might have been sullen and irritable. I would have felt he was pushing me around. On the other hand, if we turned back, I would be letting him push me around. We were really pulling wildly against each other. I knew he wanted to wring my neck, yet he acted with grace and charm. On the road again he was neither sullen nor irritable. When we got to Chartres and entered the Cathedral, again he remained with Loretto, letting me wander around by myself. It was midafternoon. Sunlight was streaming through the famous blue windows. They began to enchant me. The sculptured heads, the Old Testament figures, were all around me. It seemed to me these heads had been carved by men who regarded the prophets as contemporaries; they had brought the whole Christian past into their present. Moving around by myself, meditating on this early Medieval view of history, I heard Ernest say scornfully to Loretto, "Look at him. He doesn't even genuflect." As a convert he had been genuflecting right and left at all the proper places. Now he was looking down his nose at me. He was inviting my wife to do the same. Ernest, the expert, the one who always knew! But I was convinced he was really wondering what happened to his horse at Longchamps.

As I remember it, when we came out of the Cathedral the three of us stood together in the dusty square, looking up at the two steeples out of two Gothic periods. I said something about Henry Adams and Chartres being all of France. He didn't answer. Here again was one of Ernest's peculiar traits. While we stood there, meditating, just looking at the church, each one of us getting his fill, he expressed no enthusiasm. His handsome head raised a little, his dark eyes half closed, he looked at the church a long time, as I did too, and he kept his thoughts to himself. He didn't ask me if I had been impressed. Yet he wouldn't have brought us there if he had thought it would have been necessary to ask such a question.

Then we heard music like calliope circus music. A little fair with tents and galleries for games had been set up just beyond the square. We wandered over. At the shooting gallery Ernest said, "Come on, let's shoot. Whoever loses, pays."

For targets there were little ducks and tiny dolls set up in a row only about eight feet away from the rail where we stood with the guns. I had done a little shooting. Not much. Not since my boyhood. But we were so close to the targets, how could you miss? We each had four shots. He knocked down his four little targets. So did I. Another round. The same result. Still again. The same result. Irritated and more determined, he insisted we go on. On the twelfth round, and on my last shot, my little target tilted, swayed, then finally fell, as Ernest and I, now competing fiercely, watched breathlessly. We would have gone on all night. Grabbing my arm, Loretto cried, "You missed, Morley. You didn't really hit it," and as I turned to protest, I caught a withering look from her. Abashed, I said, "That's right," and I paid. As I glanced at Ernest I could see he felt somewhat mollified.

When we got into the car to begin the drive back to Paris, Ernest said a nearby place was famous for snails. The snails there were as good as any in France. This restaurant on the road from Chartres turned out to be a damp cellar. Snails were not my favorite dish, I said calmly, knowing I was losing all prestige. Loretto and Ernest, of course, ate the snails with great relish. "He doesn't like snails, Loretto," Ernest kept saying with too much satisfaction. Again I knew he was picking on me. Again I knew his horse at Longchamps was still in the back of his mind. Yet the fact that he had caught me failing to genuflect, his little triumph at the shooting gallery, and now the snails made him almost jolly with us. On the way back to Paris we were laughing and joking again.

It had got dark while we were still on the road. But the lights of Paris were ahead. As we drove into the suburbs Ernest grew more subdued. At the first corner he stopped the car. "I want to get a paper," he said. When he had got out, my wife said fervently, "Pray to God that horse didn't win." We saw him buying a newspaper. Breathless, we waited, watching him standing under the streetlight, scanning the track results. Then he came toward us, smiling. "Well, my horse didn't even run in the money. You saved me some dough," he said. And we laughed in our nervous relief.

He drove us home to our little hotel on Raspail. It was quite dark now. I remember so clearly our parting with him. The streetlight was on him, and in that light there seemed to be so much warmth and vitality in his face. He kissed my wife good-bye. As I shook hands with him, watching him smile, aware of all the ease and sweetness in him, I was moved, not only because it seemed to be right that the last full day I should be spending with anyone in France should be with him, but because in all our boxing afternoons when we had been pummeling each other, we had never had a harsh word. Not even when Scott got mixed up in it; and even the fierce silent little struggle with him over having my way about going on to Chartres was the kind of struggle you have with a man you feel very close to, and he had shown more grace than I would have shown myself. As we said good-bye, we assumed we would soon see him again. Then he got into his car, waved, laughed and was gone.

"I was glad he showed up the other night," I said.

"Well, I could have kicked you at that shooting gallery," Loretto said. "The guy comes around and takes us to Chartres when he wants to be at the races. You won't turn back. And then you won't even let him win a little shooting match. What's the matter with you? You said yourself the first day here with him, he just has to be champion."

CHAPTER XXVIII

Our leave-taking of the Quarter and our departure for London seemed to have been rather hurried and crowded. I'm looking now at a letter to London from Titus:

> . . . frankly I have never before seen such an experience as we had getting you off. If we had taken for granted the porter's statement that the train had gone, and had not tipped everyone right and left, you probably would not have got off. . . . I have had Hemingway up at the house the other night . . . he said he might write me an introduction to Kiki's memoirs. . . . You are very much missed.

I forget the cause of the confusion in our departure, but I remember that as soon as we got into a London taxi I knew definitely the journey was over and we were on the way home. It was the taxi driver. He was a thin grave middle-aged man wearing one of those straw boaters. I tried to make a joke with him as I would have done with a Paris taxi driver. As he looked at me with his gray, dignified, straw-hatted disapproval, he could have been taken for an alderman in my native city.

We stayed only two weeks in London. All our mornings were spent in the National Gallery where, uninvited and unnoticed, we joined an art class. The first morning, when we had been looking at a Michelangelo drawing, a middle-aged teacher with an authoritative voice had swooped down on us with a group of students, and had begun a lecture on Renaissance art. We let the group carry us along to the next subject. At noontime he said, "Well, the same time tomorrow." We were there. All that week we were members of the class, and no one asked where we came from. In London we didn't look up Helena Rubenstein, nor use any of the letters of introduction Sinclair Lewis had given us.

After two weeks we went to Ireland. In Dublin, at the Gresham Hotel, I would try to talk to the woman who managed the place about William Butler Yeats, but she would rather have talked about the big nights at the hotel when the horsey set was there. In Dublin streets, looking for Joyce's Dubliners, we would wonder if Joyce himself in Paris was still playing that Aimee Semple McPherson record. We went down to Cork and into the countryside. But Ireland only made us feel melancholy and anxious to be on our way home.

In New York when I walked into Perkins' office, I was carrying an Irish blackthorn, and he tried to hide his amusement. We talked about Ernest and Scott and he told me that Ernest had written him letters about our boxing. And I could tell he wasn't aware of Scott's humiliation.

Back in Toronto I waited for the publication of the novel *It's Never Over,* which I had written in Paris, and began to write stories. Often I would find myself wondering when Ernest and Scott would return to America. A friend of mine had told me, smiling, that Ernest in a letter had referred to me as "Lord Morley." It worried me. Granting it was an amusing view of me, it made me think of Scott trying to stand on his head to impress me. What kind of guy was I? Some men ask this question of themselves day and night. The question had never bothered me. And perhaps it was why Ernest, aware of my attitude, could jokingly refer to me as "Lord Morley."

Only a few weeks had passed since our return. Now I remember the day in November when I went into a bookstore to get the New York Sunday papers. Reading the *New York Herald Tribune* "Books," I finally came to Isabel Paterson's page, a page of gossip and chitchat about writers and publishers. My eye caught Hemingway's name, then my own. The story was about my meeting Hemingway in Paris. According to this story Hemingway, sitting at the Dôme when I came along, told me the story I had written about a prizefighter was no good; it was obvious that I knew nothing about boxing. And there and then he challenged me to a match. I had knocked him out in one round.

The story filled me with such agitation I couldn't think clearly. I called Loretto. I showed her the story. We both felt desolate. Who had put out the story? Then, stricken, I knew it didn't matter; the malicious thing had been printed, a legend very important to Hemingway might be destroyed. And what was more terrible, I knew, was that the malice struck at the root of his whole fantasy. He had been made to look like a boastful bully whose bluff had been called. A host of envious people would rejoice to have their own wishful view of him confirmed. And no matter what he had thought of me, I felt very close to him.

For some hours I couldn't get my thoughts organized. I was too full of protest. It seemed to be a ghastly outrageous irony that I had been chosen as the one who could humiliate my friend. Finally I sat down and wrote the following letter to the *Herald Tribune*:

Toronto, Nov. 26/29

DEAR MISS PATERSON,

Last Saturday I saw the story of the singular encounter between Ernest Hemingway and me, taken from the Denver *Post*. It is a fine story and you can imagine how much I regret not deserving such a reputation, but this ought to be said:

Hemingway, as far as I know, never sat at the Dôme last summer. Certainly he never sat there panning my fight stories and whatever background I might have for them. I have only written one fight story anyway. I'll have to do some more at once. Nor did I ever challenge Hemingway. Eight or nine times we went boxing last summer trying to work up a sweat and an increased eagerness for an extra glass of beer afterwards. We never had an audience. Nor did I ever knock out Hemingway. Once we had a timekeeper. If there was any kind of a remarkable performance that afternoon the timekeeper deserves the applause. Being of a peaceful and shy disposition I have only envy for strong men who challenge each other then knock each other out. But I do wish you'd correct that story or I'll never be able to go to New York again for fear of being knocked out.

Best personal wishes,

Then I wrote to Max Perkins, enclosing a copy of the letter I had written to Isabel Paterson. I knew he would understand my concern. I prayed that Ernest in Paris might not see the New York *Tribune*—at least not until my correction had appeared.

Within a week I heard from Perkins, who comforted me. My letter to the *Herald Tribune* would be printed, he said. No one would be injured, he assured me. I also got this note from Isabel Paterson:

Dec. 3, 1929

DEAR MR. CALLAGHAN,

I am printing your correction next Sunday. Sorry to have been misled, though I must admit it sounded too good to be true. If I had known you were back in Toronto I might have sent it to you to check up. I had no idea where to look for you in Paris last summer, didn't know where anyone was, and consequently saw no one which I regretted very much. I thought Ford was going to be over there and tell me about the others; but he didn't arrive back from New York until a day or so before I had come back.

Good luck.
Sincerely,
ISABEL PATERSON

But just before my letter was printed I got a cable from Scott: HAVE SEEN STORY IN HERALD TRIBUNE. ERNEST AND I AWAIT YOUR CORRECTION. SCOTT FITZGERALD.

And the cable came to me collect!

All week I had been upset, torn between melancholy and disappointment. When I got this cable from Scott I was blind with indignation. The arrogance of the cable! Scott sending it to me collect! Was I supposed to be the one who put out the story? If he wanted to correct the story why didn't he do so? Or why didn't Ernest do it himself? Scott taking it upon himself to handle the situation—a good little boy taking over for Ernest, when he knew I was aware of his own bitterness. What did he want me to do? Write the story, tell the truth, tell in detail the whole affair, tell about him crying out, "He thinks I did it on purpose"? I had expected to hear from Ernest, but not from Scott.

And when I read in the *Herald Tribune* my elegant gloss of the events in question, I felt all the more enraged. I wrote Scott a letter. Until now I had been the one untouched by rancor. My two friends might nurse their secret resentments, but I had done nothing to bring humiliation upon myself. To this day I feel ashamed of that letter I wrote to Scott. It is a humiliation to me even now to remember it. I told him it had been unnecessary for him to rush in to defend Ernest. For him to hurry out and send that cable to me collect without waiting to see what I would do was the act of a son of a bitch and I could only assume that he was drunk as usual when he sent it.

I wrote Perkins, told him of the cable from Scott, told him it enraged me.

By this time, of course, Perkins was trying to calm his insulted authors. My piece in the *Tribune* had appeared. Perkins was busy writing to Scott and to Ernest and to me.

Finally I heard from Ernest. The letter was a beauty. I have it on my desk now, dated January 4, 1929. (Actually, the thirties had begun—we weren't still in '29.) It was sent from 6 rue Ferou, in Paris. It is written in pencil.

In this letter Ernest put the blame on Pierre Loving for starting the story in both Paris and New York, and he said that he had cabled to Loving in New York saying he had heard Loving had seen him knocked out by me. But Loving hadn't replied.

And then Ernest said it was at his instigation that Scott had cabled me, calling my attention to the appearance of the story and saying he was waiting impatiently to see me cor-

rect it. In this letter Ernest underlined his acceptance of all
responsibility for the cable. Scott had acted against his own
convictions. Then Ernest went on to say that because three
weeks had passed since the story had been printed in the
New York *Post (sic)* he couldn't know whether I had seen it or
corrected it, and if I hadn't it would have fallen to Scott to
do it, since he had been present. Again Ernest repeated
Scott was against sending the cable, insisting I would have
read the story. But the wire, Ernest went on, made no reflection on me. Three weeks had elapsed before he himself had
read the story, therefore he couldn't be certain I had read it.

Again he took the entire responsibility for the sending of
the cable to me. Since some abusive language was being used
concerning the one who was responsible for the dispatch of
the wire, he was telling me Scott was blameless. He, Ernest,
was the one. If I wanted to switch to him the abusive terms
I had directed at Scott, he was coming to the States shortly
and would be at my service wherever it could be kept
private.

So Ernest wanted to meet me and knock my block off! And
I knew why. It was as he had said; he had literally compelled
Scott to send that peremptory and arrogant cable. Yes, I
could see what had happened. Upset as he should have been,
as I myself in his place would have been, he had rushed out
looking for Scott. And I could see Scott, distressed and pale,
trying to reason with him, begging him to wait. And I could
see Scott, too, under the pressure of Ernest's anger, recalling
all the embarrassment Ernest had suffered that day in the
American Club. Perhaps Scott had been made to feel half
guilty himself. And he must have wondered bitterly what
had kept driving him to ask to be allowed to come with us.
Going against his own wisdom, his own sensibility, and re-

membering that Ernest had left him feeling that he, Scott, enjoyed seeing him humiliated, Scott had given in and sent the cable. Now here was Ernest inviting me to transfer the epithets I had addressed to Scott to him. Even after reading my piece in the *Tribune,* Ernest still panted to beat me up.

I wrote to him calmly enough. I said I regretted what had happened. Then, to let him know what I thought of him for dragooning Scott into sending the cable, I wrote that I couldn't transfer the epithets to him. Since he had compelled Scott to send the cable, I would have to get a whole fresh set of epithets to address to him.

Again I heard from Perkins, who knew about the cable and who had heard from Paris. Scott had read my letter in the *Herald Tribune.* According to Perkins, Scott had tried desperately to assure Ernest that they should leave the whole matter to me. They both knew me. I was bound to see the original story and know how it would torment Ernest, and I would be quick to come to his defense. Perkins wanted me to know that from beginning to end I had acted like a little gentleman and that Scott was full of remorse. Perkins asked me to leave everything to him.

A little later I got a letter from Scott, a letter from Paris dated January 1, and he too seemed to believe we were still in the year 1929 and not 1930.

The letter is written in ink in bold clear handwriting easy to read, and I look at it now on the desk before me, and recall all my feelings. Plunging right in, Scott apologizes without any reservations for what he called his "stupid and hasty" telegram. He assures me he knew I was quick to deny the story, and he wants me to know it never entered his head that I might have started the rumor. It had never been his intention to make the telegram sound insinuating, and he was sorry for the wording of it. But with the story being repeated he felt it had to be denied by him or me, and since I was on the ground it was his idea that it was up to me. And then Scott went on to say that he himself had too often endured pain from these scandalous stories, and he believed they stayed around a long time unless they were immediately wiped from the slate.

As for the story itself and who put it out, it was his conviction it just grew spontaneously, and knowing who was the one who put the mischievous twist in it was beyond calculation. But the story as it was now, making Ernest a boastful bully who got what was coming to him, was certainly far from the source. Then Scott said that he hadn't even told Edmund Wilson or Perkins what had happened. As for me being the one who started the story, he had never even implied in any way to anyone, including Ernest, that I was remotely responsible. But he recognized that he had been gravely unjust to me and since he was returning in February he would be happy to offer his amends to me in person.

The dignified, half-formal tone of the apology shamed me. Poor Scott. Once again he was caught in the middle. As I said some time ago, he was always the one who managed to get caught in a bad light. His fineness of spirit, his generosity, all that was perceptive in him had prompted him to urge Ernest to be patient. The touch of comedy in the whole situation lay in this: they were both assuming I would or should do the job. Yet neither one of them could have wanted me to tell the truth, neither one imagined for a moment I would give a factual account of the events of that afternoon. However, Scott, having been insulted by Ernest that day in the American Club, was now insulted by me because he had acted to please Ernest. Having listened to him at the Amer-

ican Club—now after this new indignity—I knew how cynical
and bitter about Ernest he would be feeling. And beyond all
doubt I knew that even if they sometimes heard from each
other, from now on in his heart Scott had finally walked out
on Ernest.

Look what Scott's admiration for Ernest, and his eagerness
for our companionship, had led to. Why did he have to come
along? Ernest, my old friend, and I now were bristling at
each other—over Scott. Ernest was anxious to fight me. For
the sake of his dream would he keep at it until he did? But
I was nursing another humiliation. I cursed myself for not
trusting my understanding of Scott. I called myself a blind
man, a dolt lacking in all perception. I ought to have known
that Scott, of his own accord, would never have sent that
demanding cable. The irony of events kept tormenting me.
I had gone to Paris, confident that I would find there a
deepening friendship with Ernest, and a fine warm intimacy
with Scott. I had found some strange tangled relationship
between Scott and Ernest, but there had been a lot of admiration and respect, too. Out of my hopeful eager journey had
come all this shameful petty rancor and wounded vanity, and
suspicion—and a challenge to fight from Ernest!

Max Perkins was being as busy as a little bee, and I received another letter from Ernest who was now in Key West.

This letter, dated February 21, was typewritten, and as I
look at it now it seems to me that Ernest must have taken a
little time with it.

Admitting he had been really sore, he suggests that I put
myself in his place. He says he knows I wasn't to blame for
putting out the story, so I should be able to look at the matter
aside from the question of who was to blame. My denial of
the story had been quick and gracious. As for his letter to

me, he said, the facts were as he had stated them, but he hadn't intended to post that letter. It was true, as I had written, that in return for my courtesy in quickly disavowing the malice of someone engaged in baiting authors he had offered to beat me up. It was simply that he had gone berserk, he wrote.

As for the letter, and how it came to be posted when he hadn't intended to send it, he wrote that he had put it aside in his desk and had driven to Bordeaux to deliver his car to the boat. His wife, remaining behind, cleaning up things in the apartment, had come on the letter, and, thinking he had overlooked it, had mailed it.

Then he went on to say that with the letter sent, he couldn't undo it. A man can't challenge another man to do battle in a letter, then wire him and tell him to pay no attention to the letter.

He could understand I would be sore at receiving a collect wire from Paris from Scott; perhaps this was due to the wire having been sent to New York. And, too, he was aware that I had no fear of him.

Again he admits he was good and angry about the story. And then he put it up to me in this way: a syndicated piece says you encounter someone, sneer at his work, get taken up on it, and then get knocked out. How would I like it myself? To make it worse, this happened with a man whose work you have praised and tried to push and whose boxing has given you pleasure and aroused your admiration.

Naturally he had been really angry, he wrote. And then came the part of the letter that fascinated me. It was about his boxing. Asserting his friendly feeling again, he nevertheless wanted to say it was his conviction, quite aside from making it a matter of either one of us being afraid of the other, that with small gloves he could knock me out. He thought he would need about five two-minute rounds. Then he granted that along the way he would be taking plenty of popping from me; he was sure he would. This belief of his however, he wrote, wasn't to be taken as the unfriendly gesture of a man who was still sore. But if I didn't share his opinion he had no desire to go on all his life working at remaining in good condition on the possibility we might encounter each other. Therefore, if it was my wish we should lay down our arms, I should tell him so. And he sent his regards to Loretto and his good wishes for the success of my book.

At last, thank heavens, I was able to laugh. In this letter he sounded more like the boyish old Ernest, and he had admitted cheerfully that he had gone berserk. And now I was moved too, for he had reminded me how he had gone around telling people about my work, my only writing friend for so long, and how happy we had been in those Paris months, and how much I had liked him.

But he wanted me to agree he could knock me out—conceding he would take a lot of punishment. Having his own peculiar view of his life, I knew he simply had to believe it. Indeed, it was at this time in Key West that he explained to Josephine Herbst, who relayed it to me, his laughable statement, "My writing is nothing. My boxing is everything." What was I to say to him? If I agreed with him I would feel I had joined the ranks of those men who were making him unreal. I decided to tell him the truth. I wrote him a good-humored letter in which I said I had no objections at all to him thinking that he, using small gloves, could knock me out in five rounds. In fact I would want him to have this opinion. But since I had never been knocked out I was sure he would understand it was hard for me to imagine him doing it. But wasn't it the way we both should feel? So for heaven's sake, disarm. It was the last I heard from him.

I don't know what Scott and Ernest said to each other, after they returned to America. They seemed to have remained nominal friends, but they had become very cynical about each other.

Then I, who admired them both, and had liked and enjoyed their company so much, made a mistake. At the time it did not seem to be a mistake. Looking back on it I can see it is the kind of a mistake men make so often in their lives when a warm relationship has been disrupted. Perkins, whom I trusted, had told me to forget the whole thing, since he had talked to both Scott and Ernest. Both of them, he said, recognized it would be absurd to hold any resentment against me. He assured me they both had goodwill for me. Now Perkins had a talent for diplomacy in difficult human situations, and he had a kind of nobility of spirit and a fine sense of fairness. Well, I took his word for it. I left it to him. It was a mistake. There had been an arranged adjustment, but what about the friendship?

Only many years later, after brooding over it, did I realize that such wounds cannot be healed by a third party, no matter how discreet and just and full of goodwill he is. Insulted and injured people, who shake hands from a distance or write apologetic letters, find themselves lying awake at night making up little speeches, some of them angry, and the one to whom these secret little speeches are addressed in the dark never has a chance to answer. No, when there has been a sudden sharp break in a relationship the two or three who are concerned have to seek each other out, face each other quickly, talk, open their hearts to each other. Men and women, of course, shy away from revealing themselves to each other, but when they withhold too much of themselves for too long, there is soon nothing left to give. They can no longer communicate honestly. And in Paris, I'm convinced, Ernest and Scott had never really got together even in the heyday of their relationship, and then with time passing, it had got harder.

I shouldn't have let the whole thing drop. I should have met Scott as he had suggested. Instead, soothed by Perkins, I was glad to be told that I did not have to say to Scott, Yes, you should see me. I was glad to duck the encounter, for I was the one now who felt secretly ashamed. I had been guilty of misjudging and abusing him. And of course, as time passed, it became much easier for me to avoid thinking of him. The Depression had come. And the world in which Scott had been a golden dazzling figure had collapsed. All that had happened to his relationship with Ernest because of me did not seem to be important. Whenever I would think of these two men who had been my friends, I would find myself growing fascinated at the way little details, little vanities, little slights, shape all our relationships. It is these little things, not clashes over great principles, that turn people against each other. Loretto and Pauline Hemingway standing at the window. "I won't bother giving you the address if you don't intend to use it," Pauline had said, and a barrier had gone up. And the night Scott said to me, "I took your arm . . . I knew what you thought I was." . . . A man acting as time-keeper lets a round go on too long and . . . Louis Bromfield's slippers.

So when Scott's *Tender Is the Night* was published, I wrote to Perkins about the book—not to Scott. Whenever I thought of him I felt the old embarrassment. To put an end to it, one time when I was in New York I asked Perkins where Scott was and was told he was in Baltimore. I would go and see him, I said. To my surprise Perkins advised me not to go at that particular time. Zelda was mentally ill and giving Scott trouble, and Scott himself was drinking heavily; it wouldn't do me any good to see him. Now I know that in spite of Perkins I should have gone to Baltimore. Suppose I *had* found Scott alcoholic? Suppose he had been nasty to me? Hadn't I encountered him in scenes which would have startled Perkins?

As for Ernest, the little matter had been straightened out to his satisfaction. Unless I sought him out I knew I would never see him. Why didn't I? Whenever I thought of doing so, I would remember how he had brought out the gloves that first day in his living room to satisfy himself he was right in his judgment of me. And if I walked in on him, and we got talking about boxing, mightn't he feel driven, as he often seemed to be driven in other matters, to prove something to himself? I wouldn't have been able to give in. God knows what might have happened if that old sense of frustration so intolerable to him had seized him. The thought of it was unbearable to me. Yet now I can see I may have been humoring myself, humoring my view of him. But I was secretly nursing some half-hidden grievance.

But with time passing, I was learning the grim lesson that all writers who aren't just morning glories, and go on, have to learn. In the beginning the good opinion of Hemingway and Fitzgerald had helped me to feel I was not alone—even in my hometown. Having passed the morning-glory period, I had learned that you can't be sustained by the praise and admiration of a few friends. You lose them along the way anyway, and since you should always be changing and becoming something else, the friends, if they stay alive, may not stay with you. I find that people who like what I did when I was twenty-five often do not like what I do now, but I have learned that this is because they would like things to be done as they were done when they, themselves, were twenty-five or thirty—the time when they were most alive themselves. And those dreams I had of Paris—as a place—the lighted place—I had learned it had to be always in my own head, wherever I was. Sometimes in strange places I have remembered that prison chaplain who insisted that no prison should be so obviously escape proof that freedom was even beyond the imagination of the inmates. They ought to be allowed at least a condition for the comfort of their fantasies. I won't enlarge on this splendid idea.

In the late forties, Sam Putnam wrote a book called *Paris Was Our Mistress*. According to this author, after playing tennis, I challenged Ernest to a boxing bout and he knocked me out in a round. I won't say that I waited to hear from Ernest, or that I demanded a correction. I never heard from him and I didn't expect to. I was sure by this time that, as a storyteller, this version to him was imaginatively true. But at least I understood my own little grievance. I had known all along he would have to have it in this light. Anyway, Ernest, over the years, was getting lost to me in the legends. Hemingway in his prime, the man I knew in Paris, the author of the early books and *A Farewell to Arms*, was perhaps the nicest man I had ever met. I can say the same for Fitzgerald. I liked those two men. In my heart I knew Ernest couldn't possibly have turned into a swaggering, happy extrovert. How they ever got him into that light and how he put up with it, I don't know. In the good days he was a reticent man, often strangely ingrown and hidden with something sweet and gentle in him. But I was glad to hear that in the last year of his life out in Sun Valley, he talked to the photographer so affectionately about those days in Paris with Scott and me, and sent me at last his warm regards.